The Big Book of Raspberry Pi

Alison Watson

Copyright 2013 by Alison Watson

Copyright Information

DEDICATION

This book is dedicated to David Chayne, J Gibson, Anne Watson, The Raspberry Pi Foundation and the next generation of computer programmers, musicians, graphic artist, system administrators and hackers.

INTRODUCTION

Google has made a bold step forward in educating the next generation of potential computer programmers, network engineers, game developers, musicians and graphic artist by announcing that they are donating 15,000 Raspberry Pi devices to schools. So what is the Raspberry Pi and why is it such an important and definitive turning point in ICT.
In brief the Raspberry Pi is a small affordable computer that is no bigger than a credit card. The cost of this device is approximately £25. It was developed at Cambridge University, England by the Raspberry Pi Foundation. The Raspberry Pi Foundation recognised the decline in ICT skills that was being taught in schools. With this in mind this book is set to teach you about the Raspberry Pi by teaching you about the hardware that the device uses and how to use the software. It will also explain how to use the device for computer networking and will explain the uses of server applications.

You will also learn how to program the device by using a number of languages although Python will be the main choice. While you are learning about the Raspberry Pi you will also be learning about the GNU/Linux operating system which many commercial companies are using today. You will also learn common Linux system administration tasks which are used in medium and large companies. This will give you an insight on how computers, servers and devices are used in real world company enterprises.

So where is GNU/Linux used? GNU/Linux is used in routers, TV's, Blu ray players, telephone systems, laptops, PC's, watches, cars, phones and many more digital devices. You will use GNU/Linux almost every day without noticing it. As GNU/Linux is so common and widespread in the work place it makes sense that you should understand it if you want to utilise your skills and take that step forward.

This book is written from the ground up teaching the basics and lightly introducing new concepts. Some chapters particularly the programming chapters will increasing become harder as it will introduce concepts that you may be unfamiliar with. Do not worry because this book will guide you through it.

WHO IS THIS BOOK FOR?

This book is for anyone who wants to learn and understand the Raspberry Pi. It is great for students starting ICT or for someone starting a computer science course and it is ideal for anyone just getting into IT. This book also covers concepts of GNU/Linux and programming which makes it ideal for the first time user of Linux or the first time programmer.

PART 1
GETTING STARTED

CHAPTER 1 - THE RASPBERRY PI

Over the years, children, students and adults have surrendered their knowledge to computer systems, mobile devices, microwave ovens, cars, heating systems and other digital devices in exchange for ease of use. By doing so we have given up a vast amount of knowledge in understanding how ICT systems works. The lack of ICT skills was recognised by the Raspberry Pi foundation, Google and other enthusiasts and this lack of skills are not just limited to school children. Adults have also lost many skills in IT and are now button pushers. It is true that software and computers have been designed to make our lives easier but this lack of knowledge and not knowing what is happening in the box has lead us down a path of only becoming passive users. The purpose of the Raspberry Pi is to rekindle the desire to learn and increase our IT knowledge. This will also increase the user skill set when they seek employment.

The Raspberry Pi is designed to inspire and teach us how computers are programmed and how they function. The foundation believes that many children, including teenagers lack the understanding and skill set to understand how a computer functions.

Back in the early 1980's, the United Kingdom was at the forefront of computer technology and computer programming. The United Kingdom led the way in innovation, new ideas, programming and hardware design. Every school in the country was equipped with a BBC micro computer which allowed children to explore this unknown object. Even the teacher did not understand how these computers functioned. In the 1980's the BBC computer was designed to help children understand computers. From this chaos and lack of guidance for the students the children managed to succeed in learning new skills on their own. There was a desire and drive to learn computers. The 1980's was a wonderful time for home computing and almost every household owned on. The Commodore 64, Oric, ZX81 Sinclair Spectrum and the Dragon

32 had found their way into the bedrooms of many children and teenagers. Most parents did not have a clue how these things worked but they had been convinced by their children that they needed it for home work. It certainly worked for me. The home computer revolution had begun. Computer games and business software was not being written by adults but by school children in their bedrooms and during their lunch breaks at school. Children would exchange ideas about computer games and programming techniques that they had learned. The tide had turned. Children now understood a technology that the generation before them didn't. The student had become the teacher.

Most adults feared this change and those without the ability to embrace this change would be left behind. The intelligent people would see this as a blessing. A generation of children had inspired themselves without prompting. Self-education in computers without being told what to do was a wonderful freedom to have.

Back to the Future

So how does this fit with the Raspberry Pi? This is the exact intention of the Raspberry Pi but this time the same generation of children in the 1980's are now a guiding beacon for others to learn from and share their ideas. It is believed that this tiny device will spark the same revolution.

The Raspberry Pi started back in 2006 by one of the trustees, Eben Upton. He was lecturing and working in the admission department at Cambridge University and he noticed a decline in computer skills and knowledge with regards to the A level students applying for computer science courses. During the 1990's most students applying for computer science came from a background of a computer hobbyist or someone who already had an understanding and desire to learn computers and programming. The lack of IT skills followed for many years to come. A generation of students just didn't have what was required to make the difference. Adults, children and students seemed to be far more interested in social media and online computer games. Ironically, the people creating these games today had grown up learning and understanding the computers of yesterday. The gap between the generation of the 1980's and the generation that are applying to jobs and Universities today is large but not unrecoverable.

The Raspberry Pi foundation assembled a group of enthusiasts and academics to create a small affordable computer that will create the desire to learn but is fun and educational at the same time. The foundation consisted of Rob Mullins, Alan Mycroft and David Braben to name a few. Their team started to develop ideas on how to combat this skill divide. The first question they had to address was "Why had the ICT skills in schools dropped to an all-time low?" The current school curriculum was biased towards students using computer programs like Microsoft Publishing and Microsoft Word. This was a great tool at teaching a student on becoming a user of Microsoft office products but it didn't address the skills required in the real world of IT. Children needed to think differently, explore more, venture out into the unknown of computers and make mistakes instead of remembering a sequence of instructions. From these mistakes came a greater understanding.

Remembering a set of sequences doesn't make you a smarter person, it just means you have a good memory. It was problem solvers that the United Kingdom had lost.

How could the Foundation create a catalyst for learning ICT skills? After experimenting with many designs, software changes and development problems the foundation created a device that would start a chain reaction that we will all be part of. The Raspberry Pi device was here. In August 2011, the foundation released a few devices for testing. As with all new things, the Raspberry Pi had some initial problems but in early February 2012 it was ready for the public to use.

The day finally came when the Raspberry Pi went on sale and the website was overwhelmed with orders. In a matter of days the Raspberry Pi had sold out and Raspberry Pi Foundation could not meet the demand. There was a three month back log in order and the order just kept coming.

The Raspberry Pi was a complete success. This is only the beginning and you are part of it.

CHAPTER 2 - WHAT IS THE RASPBERRY PI?

The Raspberry Pi is a very cheap small computer that has some amazing features. For example it can be plugged directly into your TV, monitor or a projector. Most computers require a monitor but the Raspberry Pi breaks this tradition. Very early computers always plugged into a TV so this isn't a break through it is just re applying what made things easier in the early days.

Your Raspberry Pi can be used to watch movies at high quality, play quality audio, create music, create graphics, write programs, controls lights, browse the internet and also has the ability to play 3D games to name just a few. Like the home computers in the 1980's the Raspberry Pi can also be plugged directly into a TV.

The great thing about the Raspberry Pi is that almost all of the software available for it is free. Most PC's that you purchase require you to buy a copy of Microsoft Windows or Mac OSX but not the Raspberry Pi, although there is an optional available to do so if you chose. The low cost of the device combined with free software means that it is open to almost anyone who wants to learn but cannot always afford to do so.

CHAPTER 3 - THE RASPBERRY PI DEVICE

Now that you understand why the Raspberry Pi is needed and why you should learn it, I should give you an overview of this amazing device. The Raspberry Pi can be plugged into a TV or monitor that supports HDMI which makes it accessible to anyone with a TV. It also has the ability to connect to older type composite connections found in older TV's. These are usually the three red, yellow and white cables. The Raspberry Pi uses the ARM processor for the majority of its calculations and even though this performs at 700MHz in its default state it can be increased up to 1 GHz and beyond. Be aware that increasing the processor speed beyond 1GHz will cause the warranty to become invalid. You have been warned. ARM processors are used in small digital devices because they are extremely efficient at calculating at high speeds and they have a very low energy consumption which produces very little heat.

The Raspberry Pi does not have a hard drive like a traditional computer but instead uses an SD card for the starting up of the device and the saving data. The SD card contains the operating system, the programs and the data needed to make the Raspberry Pi useful. The operating system manages the entire system by handling input from the user, managing programs and overseeing the entire system.

A majority of the software for the Raspberry Pi uses a concept called open source. Open source can be thought of as free software which has been created so that everyone can use the software for free but also see how the software was made. It will even let you modify the software to your own needs. Other operating systems use a closed proprietary model which can limit the understanding of the software and hides the source code from the programmer. This stops the ability to extend the software in anyway and prevents you from learning how it was created.

There are a number of open source operating systems and variations that are available for the Raspberry Pi. Razdroid, OpenElec, Fedora, Arch, RiscOS Open, QtonPi, Fedora, Debian, Bodhi and more. Each individual distribution contains its own set of programs known as packages and its own way of managing the packages that are installed.

Since the Raspberry Pi first came into production it has seen some changes. One of which was a revision to the device. This was called revision 2. Revision 2 has a greater memory capability increasing revision 2 to 512MB. Revision 1 can only support 256MB of memory. To use the increased memory on revision 2 you may have to enable it.

In later chapters we will explain how to achieve 512MB of memory. The foundation also introduced a £19 model which featured fewer components.

CHAPTER 4 - HARDWARE

You can start using the Raspberry Pi without understanding the hardware involved but it is always good practice to become familiar with the components. Below is a diagram that makes up the Raspberry Pi hardware.

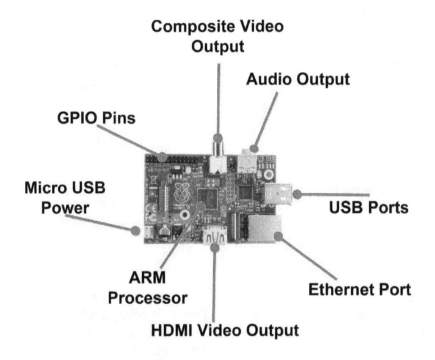

Micro USB Power Port
The micro USB power supply is used to power the device. This should only be plugged in when everything is connected. The Raspberry Pi does not have an on and off switch like most devices so to power off the device you must unplugged the micro USB power supply. Most compatible phone charger adapters will power the pi. A genuine micro usb Samsung charger will work fine.

HDMI output
To send video output the Raspberry Pi you must use either the HDMI port or the composite video output (see composite output).

Composite output
The composite video connection is used to output to older TV's and projectors.

Ethernet port
The Ethernet port is used to connect a network cable to your router or local network. This is the easiest way to get online.

USB 2.0 ports
The USB 2.0 ports are used so that you can plug in peripherals such as a keyboard, a mouse or, an external hub or a Wi-Fi adapter.

Audio output
The Raspberry Pi will output sound via the HDMI output but if you are not using the HDMI for output you will have to use a 3.5 audio cable into an external amplifier.

SD Card
The SD card must contain a working operating system so that your Raspberry Pi can start up. The operating system is a collection of software that will allow you to create files, open programs, plays music, games and manage the whole system. If you do not have an operating system image then you will need to download one. Search the web site of the Raspberry Pi Foundation to obtain an operating system.

Processor
The Raspberry Pi uses the ARM processor as the main processor but also has a GPU which is used for graphic calculations.

Memory

The memory is also located in the same location as the processor in a stacked formation.

CHAPTER 5 - THE INTERACTIVE STUFF

The great thing about the Raspberry Pi is that you can extend its functionality by adding external devices. By default you will need some way of getting information to the Raspberry Pi and this is normally done using a keyboard directly plugged into a USB port. If you intend to use the desktop you will need to use a mouse so that you can interact easily with the Raspberry Pi. Below is a list of essential peripherals that you will need to use your Raspberry Pi.

Micro USB Power Charger
A micro USB power cable is required so that you can power up the Raspberry Pi.

Keyboard
A USB keyboard is needed so that you can type commands into the Raspberry Pi.

Mouse
A mouse is required so that you can use a pointing device when interacting with the desktop.

Monitor / TV
A monitor or TV is required so that you can see the Raspberry Pi video output.

The peripherals listed below are not essential to get your device working but they will certainly extend its capability.

Optional Peripherals

Wi-Fi Adapter
If you want to connect your Raspberry Pi to a wireless network you will need to connect a Wi-Fi device. The EdiMax EW-7811 UN Wireless device which can be purchased from Amazon will work with the Raspberry Pi when it has been configured. Setting up a Wi-Fi adapter with the Raspberry Pi will be explained later.

A USB hub
One of the shortcomings of this amazing device is that the designers have only included 2 USB 2.0 ports. I am sure they had good reason for this but if you have three peripherals devices that you want to use simultaneously then you need a USB hub. You can easily extend the amount of USB ports by plugging in a powered external USB device. Doing so will only occupy 1 USB port on your device and has now added more USB ports for you to plug peripherals into. You can plug in your keyboard, mouse and additional peripherals into the external powered USB hub. I would however recommend that you only plug in your Wi-Fi adapter directly into the Raspberry Pi.

An external USB HUB.

USB Bluetooth Adapter
A Bluetooth adapter can be used to pair with a mouse or a keyboard and any other devices that support Bluetooth technology.

USB Ethernet Adapter
An external Ethernet adapter can be used to extend the amount of Ethernet ports on your Raspberry Pi.
Many other devices that extend the capabilities of the Raspberry Pi are web cams, GPS devices, TV tuners, radio devices, 3G dongles, touch screen devices and even a floppy disk drive.

Using a Bluetooth adapter which can be used for your mouse and keyboard will free up a USB port. For example if you wish to use a Wi-Fi adapter then plug in the Wi-Fi adapter into a USB port followed by the Bluetooth adapter. This will allow you to use your keyboard and mouse and also connect to a wireless network.

CHAPTER 6 - WRITING THE IMAGE

The Raspberry Pi requires an operating system so that you can start using the device. Irrelevant of the operating system that you will select the process of writing an operating system image is the same. To get started you will need a blank SD card. Use at least a 4GB SD card.

In later chapters you will follow instructions on installing Debian, Fedora and more. Each operating system can follow the same process of writing the image to the SD card.

Writing the Image on Windows XP/Vista/7/8

Download your desired operating system image from the Raspberry Pi Foundation or from any other source that provides Raspberry Pi images. Download "Win32 Disk Imager" from

http://www.softpedia.com/get/CD-DVD-Tools/Data-CD-DVD-Burning/Win32-Disk-Imager.shtml.

Extract the contents to a new folder. Double click on the icon to run Win32 Disk Imager.

Click on the blue folder icon and browse to the image file. Select your SD card device letter by clicking on the device drop down list. Your device letter may differ depending on the drive letters you have available. Check that you are writing to the SD card device. Click on the write button and wait for the image to completely write to the SD card.

Once completed remove your SD card safety and insert it into the Raspberry Pi making sure that your device is NOT powered on.

Writing the image using Mac OSX

Open a terminal and enter the command **su** to become a root user. Plug in your SD card and locate the device name by using the command

diskutil list
You will need to unmount the SD card so that we can write an image to it. Enter the command
diskutil unmountDisk /dev/diskX
Where X is the number of your disk listed in the above command.
Enter dd if= *abc.img* of=/dev/diskX
Where abc is the name of your operating system image.

Writing the image using Linux
First you need to figure out the name of the SD card device.
Open a terminal and Enter df –h and press enter.
In my case, this will display a list of devices connected.

Devices	Size	Mounted on
/dev/sda1 ....60G...............		/mnt/sda1

Insert your SD card and re issue the same command, df –f. This will display the SD card device name. Your output may differ but you can be sure by checking the size of the device.

Devices	Size	Mounted on
/dev/sdb1 ....3.8G.........		/mnt/sdb1

In order to write the image you will need to unmount the SD card. Enter the command into a terminal
umount /dev/sdb1

Go to the directory where you downloaded the operating system image and enter.

```
sudo dd if=the_debian_image_file of=/dev/sdb1 bs=1M
```

Again, your device name may differ so instead of sdb1, your device might be sdb2. It will take some time to write the image to the SD card.
When the SD write has completed remove the card and insert it into your Raspberry Pi.

CHAPTER 7 - SETTING UP THE RASPBERRY PI

The previous chapters have built up your knowledge of the Raspberry Pi but now it is time to do some practical work. This following step by step guide will simplify the process of understanding what is required in order to get the Raspberry Pi working. Follow each of the steps to connect your Raspberry Pi.

Do not plug in your power adapter until we have connected all the peripherals. The Raspberry Pi does not have an on and off switch but instead will power up as soon as you plug in the power supply. We will explain how to power on your Raspberry Pi later in this chapter.

This also makes a good checklist for beginner users and confirms the peripherals that are required to use the device.

Begin by removing the Raspberry Pi from the box.

Step 1- Plug in your SD card

Step 2- Insert your mouse into the USB port

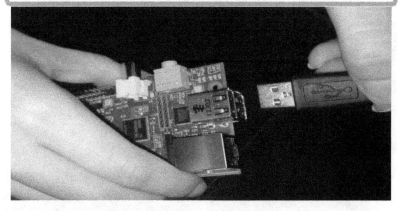

Step 4- (optional) Plug in your CAT 5 network cable

If you want to use the internet and most of our examples will then you must use a Wi-Fi adapter or an Ethernet cable.

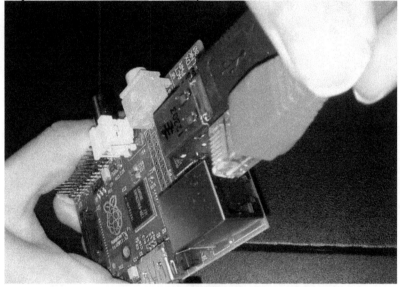

If your monitor or TV does not support HDMI input then you can use a composite cable to connect to the TV.

Additional information

If you do have a wireless adapter then we recommend that this is plugged directly into your Raspberry Pi. The reason for this is that when using some wireless devices it is known to cause problems when plugged in via the HUB. This does however cause a one of the USB ports to be taken. In order to use both the mouse and keyboard you will need to use an external USB hub of use a wireless mouse and keyboard.
To use a wireless mouse and keyboard simply plug in the wireless device for the mouse and keyboard into one of the USB ports and turn on your mouse and keyboard.

You are now free to plug in your Wi-Fi adapter or another peripheral that uses a USB port.

If you are using an HDMI connection then the audio will default to your TV or monitor. If you are using a composite connection to an older TV, you will need to plug your audio cable into an external speaker.

If you are using a wired connection to connect to the internet you will need an Ethernet network cable.
To summerise you will need the following to get your Raspberry Pi working.

1. The Raspberry Pi.

2. Micro USB power charger.

3. USB Keyboard.

4. USB Mouse.

5. HDMI cable or a composite cable for older TV's.

6. SD card containing a valid operating system.

7. TV or monitor.

PART II
THE OPERATING SYSTEMS

CHAPTER 8 - AN OVERVIEW OF DEBIAN

Assuming that you have installed an operating system to the SD you should now power up the Raspberry Pi. If not refer to chapter 4 Depending on the operating system you have installed will depend on the different scenarios that you are presented with.

The Gnu/Linux Debian operating system will be explained first by running through a typical Debian boot sequence. The Raspberry Pi will power up and your screen may display an array of colours. This screen will disappear leaving you with a vast amount of scrolling text. Some distributions may not have a colourful screen to start with and will start to display scrolling messages from the outset. You may be left with a terminal prompting you to login or your Raspberry Pi may boot directly into the desktop. If this is the case you will need to start your desktop.

Login to your Raspberry Pi and enter startx at the terminal and press enter. This command will start your desktop. LXDE is a desktop that many distributions use for the Raspberry Pi. LXDE is lightweight and is designed to run effectively and efficiently on smaller devices. The LXDE desktop was created to make the user experience easier and more intuitive. One of the most important features of the desktop is the file manager. The file manager allows you to view, copy, create, delete and modify files and gives you the ability to navigate the whole file system easily.

Left click on the icon to the left of the globe to open a window containing your home files. Your files will be saved in your home directory which is stored in the "/home/your-user-name folder".

Close the window by clicking on the top right X.

The simplest way to get your Raspberry Pi on the internet is to plug a network cable or CAT-5 cable into your device and plug this cable directly into your router or network point.

Setting up a Wi-Fi adapter
The wpa-gui application will allow you to scan for wireless networks and connect to them using the interface. When your preferred network is found you simply select it and enter your wireless password.

Install wpa-gui and go to the LXDE menu and select the 'Internet' item and left click your mouse button on the 'wpa-gui'. Click on the scan button to display a results dialog box. Click on the second scan button.

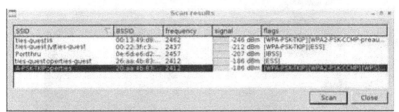

Select the wireless network that you want to connect to by double clicking on a preferred network. On the next dialog box enter your wireless password in the PSK text box and click on the '*Add*' button. Click the close button on the 'Scan results' dialog box. The current status tab will display '*Completed (station)*' when you are connected.
Click on the globe to open a web browser. This will give you access to a web browser. You can also access the internet from the programs menu. When you click on this icon the Midori web browser will open. Midori has been created to be fast and lightweight.

The Taskbar
The taskbar is located at the bottom of your desktop which gives you access a number of programs and quick access to common tasks.

The LXDE icon which is located on the bottom left of your desktop will give you access to the programs installed on your Raspberry Pi. Click your mouse button to view the programs that are installed. Depending on the distribution it may have a different window manager and will therefore contain different menus.
A program that you will need to be familiar with is the terminal. The terminal can be found in all distributions. Left click the 'LXTerminal' menu icon which can be found in the accessories menu item.

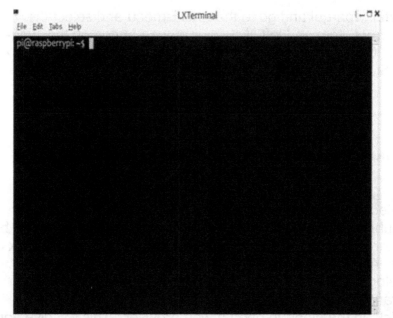

Using the terminal will allow you to enter commands and view output from the operating system. Type the command **exit** to close the terminal.

One feature that is essential is the shutting down of the device. Left click the mouse button on the red power icon at the bottom right hand corner of your desktop. The next screen presents you with a number of options from shutting down the device to rebooting. Click on the shutdown button to shutdown the device. When the Raspberry Pi has shut down the screen will turn black.

You can also shutdown the device from a terminal window by entering the following.

$ sudo shutdown -h 0

The SD card and the file system layout

Now is a good time to explain how the operating system is structured. The SD card is needed to load the operating system which will allow you to perform actions using your Raspberry Pi. There are a number of files and folders on the SD card which are used by the operating system which include the booting process, the processing of user information, managing physical devices and more. The top of the structure is known as the root file system and is indicated as a forward slash '/'. Below this you will see a number of folders including boot, bin, home and so forth.

```
                              /


boot bin dev etc home lib lost+found media mnt opt proc sbin selinux sys tmp usr var
```

Enter the following command in a terminal window and press enter.

$ ls /
'/' This is the root directory which contains all the folders listed below.

'*boot*' folder contains information that is required to start or boot up the Raspberry Pi.

'*bin*' contains binary files that are required to run the Raspberry Pi. Most common commands used by users are located here.

'dev' contains information on the devices that are connected to your Raspberry Pi such as the HDMI device.

'*etc*' contains system configuration files that are required by programs and also contains startup and shutdown scripts to start and stop programs.

'*home*' contains a folder for each user added to the Raspberry Pi. By default the '*pi*' user account already exists in the 'home' folder.

'*lib*' contains programs that are shared with different applications throughout the system. Many programs use the libraries in this folder.

'lost+found' will store data if your Raspberry Pi crashes. '*media*' will contain a special area for storage devices such as CD drives and memory sticks.

'*mnt*' will give you access to external storage devices such as external hard drives.

'*opt*' contains software that is not part of the operating system.

'*proc*' is a special virtual directory containing text information regarding which system resources are being used.

'*selinux*' contains a collection of programs designed with security features in mind.

'*sbin*' contains binary files that are designed to be invoked by the root user or by using the sudo command. Files in this folder are for maintaining the system.

'sys' contains more operating system related files.

'tmp' as hinted by the name is used to store temporary files by the system and applications. When the system is rebooted the files that have been created will be erased.

'usr' is used to store programs that can be accessed by a user.

'var' contains variable files and is used by applications in which files grow and shrink in size. A database or log files will be placed here.

CHAPTER 9 - CONFIGURATION

You can make changes to the Debian Wheezy distribution by using the raspi-config tool. This tool allows you to change a number of settings. Using a terminal enter raspi-config.

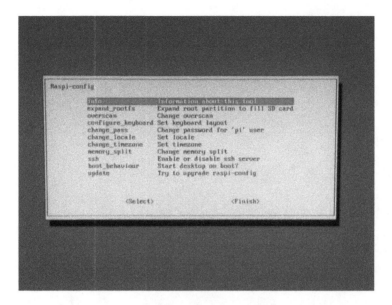

The info menu item displays information about Raspi-config. The Expand_rootfs tool will be used to fill the entire space on the SD card. The configure keyboard is used to select your keyboard configuration. Change_pass is used to change your password and the Change_local tool allows you to change language and country settings. Change_timezone allows you to modify your time zone. The Memory_split tool is used to distribute the memory between the ARM processor and the GPU.

Overclocking is used to force the processor to run faster and in some cases up to 50%. The Raspberry Pi runs at a speed of 700Mhz and the overclocking feature allows the device to run at speeds of up to 1Ghz. The impact of this will cause your Raspberry Pi to run at higher temperatures and can cause the life span of the device to decrease overtime. If you chose to overclock the device and at any time and you are unable to boot your Raspberry Pi simply hold down the shift key when booting. This will disable the overclocking feature. The SSH menu item can be enabled to allow remote access to the Raspberry Pi. The boot_behaviour item allows you to boot directly to the desktop or directly to a terminal. The update tool is used to apply any updates available.

The Raspberry Pi foundation released an updated version of the Raspberry Pi and this is called Revision 2. Revision 2 allows you to increase the memory to 512MB and there are number of ways to do this. Depending on how new the operating system is then it may automatically use the 512MB of memory.

The simplest method is to issue the following commands.

$ sudo apt-get update
$ sudo apt-get upgrade

When the updates are completed you can run raspi-config to modify your memory split between the GPU and the ARM processor. Enter the following.

$ sudo raspi-config

Go to the memory_split option and press enter. The next screen asks you to allocate how much memory you would like to assign to the GPU. Depending on your memory requirements for the GPU you will need to enter a number here for example enter 64. This will allocate 64MB to the GPU chip. When you have applied the changes you will be asked to reboot the device. You can check that the memory settings have been applied by viewing the /boot/config.txt file.

$ cat /boot/config.txt

The line that is configuring your GPU memory is

gpu_mem=64

This line indicates that 64MB of memory have been allocated to the GPU.

To check the total memory on your Raspberry Pi, enter the following.

$ cat /proc/meminfo | grep MemTotal

If you want to view how much memory is available, enter the following.

$ cat /proc/meminfo | grep MemFree

If you are using another distribution then you may need to manually copy the files over to your SD card.

One way to do this is to use a PC or Mac to download the files and copy them to the SD card or you can download them directly to your Raspberry Pi. In either case the file locations to copy the downloaded files are the same. To increase the memory on your Raspberry Pi follow the instructions below. Go to the following web site and download the arm384_start.elf file by clicking on the raw file button.

https://github.com/raspberrypi/firmware/blob/164b0fe2b3b56081c7510df93bc1440aebe45f7e/boot/arm384_start.elf

Copy the arm384_start.elf file to the /boot directory. You also need to rename this file to self.elf. Download the fixup.dat file by also clicking on the raw button.

https://github.com/raspberrypi/firmware/blob/c57ea9dd367f12bf4fb41b7b86806a2dc6281176/boot/fixup.dat

Copy fixup.dat to the /boot directory. Modify config.txt by adding

gpu_mem=64

This means that the GPU will use 64MB of memory and the remainder will be used by the ARM processor.

CHAPTER 10 - INSTALLING PACKAGES

Installing packages on your Raspberry Pi is a simple process of selecting the packages you want to install. The device will then download the package from the internet. A package is a compressed file archive containing files that make up a program. In a terminal enter

$ sudo apt-get install synaptic

The screen will fill with information related to the installation of the package. The apt-get program is used to install packages from a terminal. The above command uses apt-get to install a program called synaptic. Synaptic is a graphical package manager which can be used within LXDE. Left click on the program menu icon and move the mouse to the preferences item and select "Synaptic Package Manager".

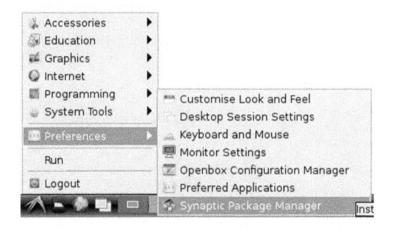

Enter your password and when the synaptic package manager appears select a category. This will display a list of packages. Select a package to install by checking a box next to the desired package. Click "mark for installation" and then click the apply button followed by the second apply button. Click OK when the installation has finished.

To remove packages from your synaptic repeat the process as above but when you click an installed package, it will display a red cross. This means that the package has been marked for removal. To remove a package using the terminal, enter the following.

$ sudo apt-get remove synaptic

Some common day to day administration tasks are listed below. To change your password, enter the following command.

$ sudo passwd

To change the password of another user called pi enter the following.

$ sudo passwd pi

To create a user account, enter the following.

```
$ sudo useradd bert
```

To bring down the Ethernet interface enter the following.

```
$ sudo ifdown eth0
```

To enable the Ethernet interface type the follow.

```
$ sudo ifup eth0
```

To display a list of interfaces connected to your Raspberry Pi enter the following.

```
$ sudo ifconfig -a
```

CHAPTER 11 - Apache, MySql, PHP & Wordpress

We will take you through a number of applications installed on your Raspberry Pi and explain what they are used for. We will explain the Nano program first as this program is used to edit many of the configuration files.

Nano
Nano is a very fast text editing program. This is very useful when editing configuration files on your Raspberry Pi.

The example below will start nano.
$ nano

You can also start nano followed by a file name. This has the effect of creating a file when you press enter.

$ nano filename.txt

You are now inside the text editor. You can see a number of options at the bottom of the screen such as ^G Get Help, ^X Exit etc. These options can be invoked by holding down the control key and pressing the letter relating to the option displayed. For example by holding down shift and pressing the 'X' key will cause nano to exit. Enter your name into the editor. Hold down the control key and press 'X'. A message is displayed explaining that you are saving the file.

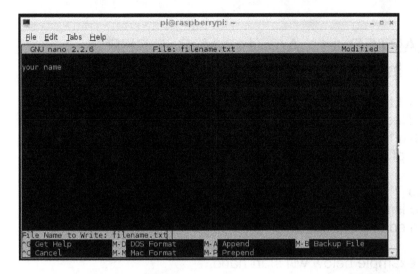

Press 'y' to save the file. Another message is displayed asking you if you want to save the file name as '*filename.txt*'. At this stage you can always save the file using a different name. Press enter to save the file using the existing file name.

You have now created a text file called '*filename.txt*'.

Apache

Apache is a web server that can be used to display web pages. It can utilise programming languages such as PHP, Ruby etc. These programming languages can be used in a web page to connect to databases and to create dynamic content.

The following steps we will guide you through the process of installing a web server and viewing a basic web page to prove that Apache is working. We will test that PHP has been installed correcting by creating a simple php web page that will display information about apache and php.

Open a terminal window and enter the following.

$ sudo apt-get update

Press 'y' to update when prompted and enter the following on one line and press enter.

$ sudo apt-get install apache2 php5 php5-mysql mysql-server

Press 'y' to continue.

During the installation process you will be prompted to enter a password for the MySql root account. This root account is allowed to make changes to MySql that regular users can't. Enter a password for the MySql account and press enter. Confirm your password by re-entering it into the text box and press enter.

Remember: You will need this password later so you may want to use something that you can remember.
Open a web browser and enter the following in the address bar of the browser.

http://localhost

This screen confirms that the web server is up and running and can display web pages. The next step is to confirm that php is working correctly.

If a timeout error appears in your web browser then it may be that the web server has not started. Enter the following to start the web server.

$ sudo /etc/init.d/apache2 start

Enter the following command.

$ sudo nano /var/www/test.php

Enter the following into the nano editor.

```
<?php
phpinfo();
?>
```

This is php code that will display information confirming that php is functioning as planned.

Enter the following into the address bar.

http://localhost/test.php

PHP Version 5.3.3-7

System	Linux raspberrypi 3.1.9+ #90 Wed Apr 18 18:23:05 BST 2012 armv6l
Build Date	Feb 10 2012 14:43:43
Server API	Apache 2.0 Handler
Virtual Directory Support	disabled
Configuration File (php.ini) Path	/etc/php5/apache2
Loaded Configuration File	/etc/php5/apache2/php.ini
Scan this dir for additional .ini files	/etc/php5/apache2/conf.d
Additional .ini files parsed	/etc/php5/apache2/conf.d/pdo.ini, /etc/php5/apache2/conf.d/suhosin.ini
PHP API	20090626
PHP Extension	20090626
Zend Extension	220090626
Zend Extension Build	API220090626,NTS
PHP Extension Build	API20090626,NTS
Debug Build	no
Thread Safety	disabled
Zend Memory Manager	enabled
Zend Multibyte Support	disabled
IPv6 Support	enabled
Registered PHP Streams	https, ftps, compress.zlib, compress.bzip2, php, file, glob, data, http, ftp, phar, zip
Registered Stream Socket Transports	tcp, udp, unix, udg, ssl, sslv3, sslv2, tls
Registered Stream Filters	zlib.*, bzip2.*, convert.iconv.*, string.rot13, string.toupper, string.tolower, string.strip_tags, convert.*, consumed, dechunk

The screenshot above displays information informing you that php has been installed on your Raspberry Pi. This page also displays any modules that you have installed such as the MySql module which will be used by WordPress.

WordPress

WordPress is a web based content management system that makes web page creation and management easy. It uses theme templates and forms to create web pages rather than writing technical web pages from scratch, although this ability is available if you want to extend WordPress.

In order to install WordPress you must first have the Apache web server, PHP and MySql need to be installed. If you have followed the instructions above then you already have what you need.

Enter the following to install WordPress.

$ sudo apt-get install wordpress

WordPress installs the required files in a folder located at /usr/share/wordpress. By default Apache does not look in this folder to install web pages so we have to make a modification.

Enter the following and press enter

$ sudo ln -s /usr/share/wordpress /var/www/wordpress

This links the /usr/share/wordpress folder to the folder in /var/www/wordpress so that apache can view the WordPress installation files.

Enter the following command and press enter.
$ sudo gunzip /usr/share/doc/wordpress/examples/setup-mysql.gz
And enter the following on one line and press enter to setup WordPress.

$ sudo bash /usr/share/doc/wordpress/examples/setup-mysql -n wordpress localhost

When the setup file has finished open a web browser and enter the following address in the web browser.

http://localhost/wordpress

You will be presented with a WordPress welcome screen. Enter a web site name in the 'Site Title' field but leave the 'Username' field as 'admin'. Enter a password in the password text field and again in the confirmation text box. This username and password will be used when logging into WordPress.

Enter your email address in the next text field and click the 'Install WordPress' button. Installing WordPress may take a few minutes to install and may give the impression that it has frozen but be patient as it takes a few minutes to install. When WordPress has installed you will be presented with a confirmation page informing you that the installation was successful.

You can login into WordPress by clicking the login button, entering the username of 'Admin' and your password that you entered during the installation. If you need to log in to WordPress in the future you can enter the following web address in your web browser.

http://localhost/wordpress/wp-admin

You can view the default WordPress web site by entering the following in a web browser.

http://localhost/wordpress

WordPress can fill an entire book alone and it has. There are a number of books available for WordPress and if you are serious about learning web site design then you should purchase a book on the subject.

CHAPTER 12 - INSTALLING FEDORA REMIX

Fedora has an alternative method of writing to the operating system to the SD card. The previous method of writing the image to the SD card will still work but the following example is far simpler. The Fedora remix image can be found using the following link. The current version is Fedora Remix 18 which can be found here using the following Uri.

http://scotland.proximity.on.ca/raspberrypi/raspberrypi-fedora-remix/18/images/.

A 4GB SD will work perfectly but if you intend to install further programs and store any data you should use a larger card. The next step is to write the image. The simplest way to do this is to download the Fedora Remix installer by Jon Chiapetta which can be found by downloading the appropriate installer for Microsoft Windows.

http://files.velocix.com/c1410/fedora/installer/windows/fedora-arm-installer-1.0.0.zip

Insert your SD card into your PC or laptop. Click on the refresh icon next to the source drop down list. This will obtain a list or images available. At this stage you can either select the image from the drop down list or browse to the image you have downloaded. Select the SD card device in the destination drop down list that you want to write the image to.

Make sure you write to the correct device otherwise you could possibly overwrite any data on that device. When you are confident you have the correct device to write to click on the 'Install' button.

When this has completed remove that SD card and insert it into the Raspberry Pi and power up the Raspberry Pi. When the Raspberry Pi is booting up for the first time a spinning Fedora icon will appear followed by the licensing information. Click on the *forward* button. Select your keyboard setting and click on the *forward* button.

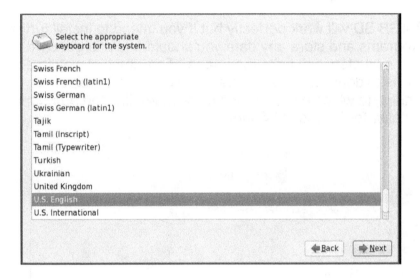

The next screen is asking you to create a user. Enter the full name of the user followed by the user name and password. You can also add this user to the *administrators* group. Check this checkbox to allow this user to perform administration tasks.

Click on the forward button. Enter the root password. This root password is used to perform system administration tasks. Click on the *forward* button. Select your time zone by clicking on a map location and click on the *forward* button.

Accept the default time servers and click on the *forward* button. Leave the default swap size on the file system settings and click on the *forward* button. Next you are asked to set a hostname. The host name is the name that you want to give to your Raspberry Pi so that it can be found on a network. For now just use the default setting of raspi.local. You can leave the settings as they are and click on the *finish* button.

After a few minutes you will be left at the Fedora login screen. Click on the drop down menu that appears and select the user name that was created during the setup.

Enter your password and click on the login button. You background may differ depending on which version of Fedora remix you are using.

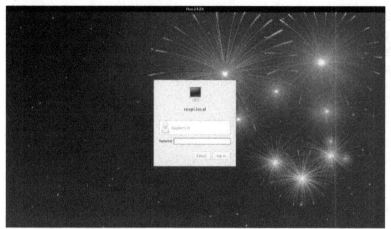

You will only need to go through this set up once. Every time you boot up your Raspberry you will be presented with this login screen.

When you have entered your login details you will be presented with a welcome message informing you that this is the first start of the panel.

You have two options "*Use default config*" and "*One empty panel*". Click on the '*Use default config*' button.

The installation procedure is painless and only takes a few steps. There are some advanced settings that you can use to modify Fedora remix which will be explored later.

CHAPTER 13 - USING THE XFCE DESKTOP

Fedora Remix uses the xfce window manager as the default desktop. Xfce is a collection of tools gathered to create a fully featured desktop environment.

A quick overview of the desktop programs include:

Window Manager (xfwm4)
This manages the windows on the desktop.

Panel (xfce4-panel)
The panel is used to dock and launch your programs.

File Manager (thunar)
The thunar file manager allows you to easily manage files throughout the file system.

Setting System (xfce4-settings)
This tool controls the appearance, display, keyboard and mouse settings.

Application finder (xfce4-appfinder)
Displays the applications installed in easy to find categories

The Desktop
The applications menu located in the top left corner contains programs that are installed on the system. Here you will find system settings including network connections, appearance and display settings along with administration applications for managing users.

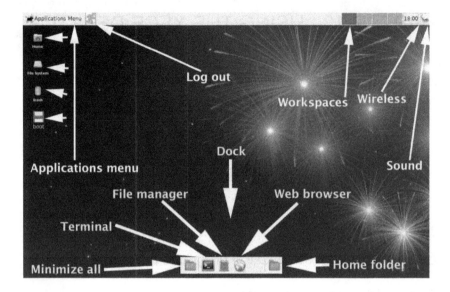

Logout

You can log out of the desktop session by clicking on this icon. This will allow you to save your current session and return to it later.

Workspace

Workspaces allow you to manage multiple desktop screens called workspaces. This is very helpful if you are working on multiple projects. On workspace 1 you can use applications that are for graphics only and on another workspace you can use programming applications. Each workspace will not interfere with the next one and makes it easy to organise your desktop.

Networks

The network icon displays networking information. You can click on this icon to display a list of networks available including wireless networks. To connect to a network click on the network name and enter the network password.

Sound

This controls sound on Fedora. Click on this icon to display the Alsa mixer sound options. If the sound isn't enabled click on 'Select Controls' and select the PCM checkbox from the dialog window. You can also control the volume from here.

Home folder icon

The home folder icon contains instant access to the files located in your home directory.

The file system

This icon provides you with direct access to the file system folders.

The trash

The trash icon is used to temporary delete files.

The boot icon

The boot icon gives you instant access to the /boot directory. From here you can modify the config.txt which contains boot up information including memory split options, display settings and other settings.

The Dock

The dock provides quick access to the file manager, the terminal, a web browser and it will allow you to minimize all windows instantly to reveal the desktop. Click on the world icon to launch a web browser. If this is the first time you have clicked on this icon it will ask you for a preferred web browser. The Midori browser is already installed by default so you associate this web browser by selecting the "No application selected" drop down and select Midori.

Application Finder

The application finder is used to locate programs and launch programs.

Popup Menus
The pop up menu gives you access to quick actions. These can be accessed by right clicking your mouse on the desktop.

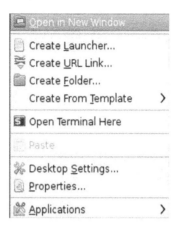

This will display a menu with a host of options from creating folders, opening a terminal window or adjusting your desktop settings. You also have access to the applications menu from here.

You can also use the middle button of a mouse to display a pop up window that provides access to the workspaces. Workspaces allow you to organise your open programs into related sessions.

For example you may be programming a game and on the first workspace you have all your programming applications, the second workspace for graphics work and third maybe dedicated to music and audio applications. The fourth can be a mixture of office, email and web browser activity.

Adding Items
You can add items to the dock by right clicking on the dock and clicking '+Add New Items'. Click on the *clock* plugin and click on the '+Add' button. You should see the clock plugin appear. Click on the close button. To remove a plugin right click the left mouse button and select remove. You can also add new items to the top panel by using the same procedure.

User and Groups

'*Users and groups*' contain permissions that allow a user access to certain files, folders and access to login to your Raspberry Pi. The '*users and group*' program can be located by clicking the mouse button on the '*Applications Menu*' and select the 'Users and Groups' item.

You will be prompted to enter your password because you are about to perform a system administration action. Enter your password to continue. The user manager window will appear. From this menu you will be able to add new users and groups. You should see your existing details are already displayed.

The first thing that you will need to do is to get your Raspberry Pi connected to the internet. When it is connected you will be able to update your version of Fedora remix. The simplest way to do this is to connect a network cable to the Ethernet port on the Raspberry Pi and plug the other end into a router. Fedora remix is configured to automatically connect to your network assuming that you are running DHCP on your network. DHCP is a way of allocating a network IP address to your Raspberry Pi and this network address is used to identify the Raspberry Pi on a network.

To update Fedora remix click your mouse button on the terminal icon located at in the dock.

$ su -

Press enter. You will be prompted to enter your password.
The prompt will change from a $ symbol to a # symbol. Enter
the following and press enter.

 # yum -y update

Enter your password when prompted to do so and press enter.
This will update the software packages and bring your Fedora
remix up to date. You should see lots of information regarding
package information appearing in the terminal window. This
may take some time but when it has finished you will be back
at the # prompt.

The YUM program is used to manage the software packages
installed on Fedora remix. We will revisit yum later and
explain what the commands are but for now just follow the
instructions.

If you have a Wi-Fi adapter you may want to use this instead.
Insert your Wi-Fi adapter and follow the instructions below.

Left click the mouse button on the icon shown below.

Your wireless network should appear assuming that you have a wireless network within range. Click your mouse button on your wireless network. You will be presented with a window requiring a wireless network password. Enter your network password and click on the connect button. The icon in the top right corner will start to spin until it has connected.

When you are connected to your network the wireless icon will change to the icon below.

Open a web browser by clicking on the world icon which is located in the centre of the screen.

You will be presented with dialog box asking you to select a preferred application.

Select the drop down box and select the Midori option.

This will open the Midori web browser and the Fedora Project web page will be displayed. You have successfully configured Fedora to go online.

You should have a basic understanding of the desktop and the Raspberry Pi by now. The next chapter will dive into the command line interface which will give you a better understanding of commands and how to use them.

CHAPTER 14 - UNDERSTANDING THE COMMAND LINE

The shell offers an alternative way to use your device and in some circumstances may be the only option available when you want to interact with it. If you have already logged into the Raspberry Pi desktop then you will need to open a terminal. Click the mouse button on the *Terminal* icon located in the dock.

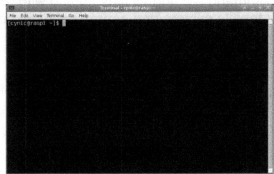

Enter the following command and press enter.

$ echo "Hello Raspberry Pi"

The echo command will print anything entered between the quotes.

$ ls

This will list the files and folders in the current directory. You can also use an asterisk which is used as a wildcard. This will display any file name that ends with .txt.

$ ls *.txt

Commands can also be combined into one line. Enter the following.

$ ls | wc -l

This command will display the number of files in the current directory. The next command will start with the sudo command. This command informs the command line that you want to execute this command as a super user. The reason for this is that we want to search all directories including those that have root permissions only.

$ sudo find / -name *.txt

The above command will find all files ending with .txt starting at the root of the file system and searching every directory.

$ cat mylist.txt

The cat command is used to display the contents of a file. In the above example the mylist.txt file will be displayed.

$ cd /var

The cd command is used to change to a directory. In the example above we have changed to the var directory.

$ pwd

Navigating through the file system can sometimes leave you a little lost. To determine your current directory enter pwd. This will show you the absolute path of the directory for example, entering the command above may return /var/log. This indicates that we are in the log directory below the var directory.

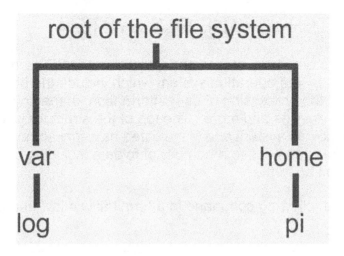

CHAPTER 15 - THE FILE SYSTEM

There are a number of files and folders on the SD card which are used by the operating system which include the booting process, the processing of user information, managing physical devices and more. The top of the structure is known as the root file system and is indicated as a forward slash '/'. Below this you will see a number of folders including boot, bin, home and so forth.

Enter the following command in a terminal window and press enter.

```
$ ls /
```

'/' This is the root directory which contains all the folders listed below.

'*boot*' folder contains information that is required to start or boot up the Raspberry Pi.

'*bin*' contains binary files that are required to run the Raspberry Pi. Most common commands used by users are located here.

'*dev*' contains information on the devices that are connected to your Raspberry Pi such as the HDMI device.

'*etc*' contains system configuration files that are required by programs and also contains startup and shutdown scripts to start and stop programs.

'*home*' contains a folder for each user added to the Raspberry Pi.

'*lib*' contains programs that are shared with different applications throughout the system. Many programs use the libraries in this folder.

'lost+found' will store data if your Raspberry Pi crashes.

'*media*' will contain a special area for storage devices such as CD drives and memory sticks.

'*mnt*' will give you access to external storage devices such as external hard drives.

'*opt*' contains software that is not part of the operating system.

'*proc*' is a special virtual directory containing text information regarding which system resources are being used.

'*sbin*' contains binary files that are designed to be invoked by the root user or by using the sudo command. Files in this folder are for maintaining the system.

'sys' contains more operating system related files.

'tmp' as hinted by the name is used to store temporary files by the system and applications. When the system is rebooted the files that have been created will be erased.

'usr' is used to store programs that can be accessed by a user.

'var' contains variable files and is used by applications in which files grow and shrink in size. A database or log files will be placed here.

CHAPTER 16 - PACKAGE MANAGEMENT

One of the first things you will want to do with Fedora will be to install new software packages. Fedora remix uses RPM packages with the YUM package manager. The YUM package manager provides you with a tool for managing programs. It gives you access to a database of all the software that can be installed on the system and also allows you to install, delete and modify software packages. YUM will require an internet connection when adding software packages as it will install the packages via the Fedora software repositories which are located online.

YUM takes the follow format.

yum install package-name

You will be installing packages as an administrator or root user which means you will have the potential to destroy important files and possibly stop the operating system from functioning. It is only recommended that you perform system administration as a root user. Enter the following.

```
$ su -
```

Enter your password when prompted. You will notice that the $ symbol has changed to a # symbol. This is informing you that you are now an administrator user.

To update a package you will use the following.

```
# yum update package-name
```

If you need to search for a package name enter the following.

```
#  yum list package-name
```

Alternatively if you only know part of the package name that you are searching for you can use the following.

```
# yum list "*google*"
```

If you need to display information about a package use the following.

```
# yum info package-name
```

You will also need to remove packages when they are no longer needed. To do this, enter the following.

```
# yum remove "package-name"
```

Using the command line is great but when you have access to a desktop environment it can be easier to use a GUI program. Synaptic is an easy to use graphical package manager. First you will need to install Synaptic from the command line interface by entering the following commands.

```
# yum install synaptic
```

The Synaptic package will download and install. After the package has been installed you will be able to locate the icon in the 'Applications Menu→Synaptic Package Manager'

The synaptic package manager will appear and you will be presented with a number of options. The panel that appears on the left contains a category listing of packages that are available for your Raspberry Pi. To the right of this located in the top panel you can find the actual package names, below this is the description of the package. Above these panels are shortcut icons and a menu containing various settings relating to the package manager and package management.

Go ahead and move your mouse over the 'Editors' category and left click your mouse button on this entry.

In the panel on the right that contains the packages, left click your mouse button on the checkbox entry that is called 'Abiword'. When the pop up menu appears click the entry that is shown 'Mark for installation'. When you select this option another menu will appear informing you that it will install additional packages. Go ahead and select the button that is labelled 'Mark'.

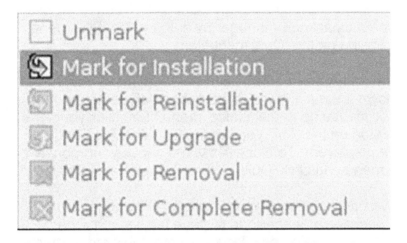

You will notice that some of the package entries are highlighted in green. This is indicating the packages that will be installed. Left click your mouse button on the green icon at the top labelled, 'Apply'. The message box is displayed informing you of the packages that will be installed. Left click your mouse button on the green 'Apply' icon.

S	Package	Installed Version	Latest Version	Description
🗹	abiword		2.9.2+svn2012040(	efficient, featureful word processor
🗹	abiword-common		2.9.2+svn2012040(	efficient, featureful word processor
🗹	abiword-plugin-grammar		2.9.2+svn2012040(	grammar checking plugin for AbiWi
🗹	abiword-plugin-mathview		2.9.2+svn2012040(	equation editor plugin for AbiWord
☐	alpine-pico		2.02+dfsg-1	Simple text editor from Alpine, a te
☐	aoeui		1.6~dfsg-2	lightweight, unobtrusive, Dvorak-op
☐	apel		10.8-2	portable library for emacsen
☐	bbe		0.2.2-1	sed-like editor for binary files
☐	beav		1:1.40-18	binary editor and viewer
☐	bhl		1.7.3-2	Emacs mode for converting annota

A window will appear showing you the progress of the installation. This may take a few minutes to install but when it has completed go ahead and left click the 'OK' button. Close down Synaptic package manager by going to the 'File' menu and left clicking on the 'Quit' menu item.

To confirm that Abi Word has been installed, move your mouse down the main menu in the bottom left corner and move your mouse up to the 'Office' menu. Left click your mouse button on the 'Abi Word' menu item and Abi Word should be displayed. To close Abi Word, move your mouse to the 'File' menu and click 'Quit'.

To remove packages from your Raspberry Pi open the synaptic package manager and click on the 'search' icon. When the search dialog box appears, enter 'abiword'. After a few moments you will see that the top panel has changed and is displaying package information relating to Abiword. Left click your mouse button on the checkbox next to 'Abiword', a menu is displayed giving you a list of options. select 'Mark for removal'.

Go ahead and click on the green 'Mark' button.

You should notice that 'Abiword' has a red cross before the package name and is now highlighted in red. This indicates that the package has been marked for removal. Select the green 'Apply' icon at the top of synaptic to begin removing the package.

Select the green 'Apply' to confirm the removal of the package.

Left click your mouse button on the 'Close' button. When the synaptic package has finished updating its information move your mouse button the 'File' menu and left click your mouse button on the 'Quit' menu item.

CHAPTER 17 - USING PROGRAMS

We will take you through a number of applications installed on your Raspberry Pi and explain what they are used for. This is not an in-depth description of how they are used and we will only show you a brief introduction to each application.

FTP is a great way to transfer files from one computer to another over the internet. To do this you will need to install an FTP client and connect to an FTP server. Open a terminal and enter the following commands.

```
$ su -

<enter your password when asked to do so and press
enter>

#  yum install filezilla
```

To start FileZilla go to 'Applications->Internet→FileZilla'.

From the FileZilla application you are able to enter a host
to connect to, the username and the password. The host
will be the server that is storing a file for retrieval. In the
host text box enter the following.

ftp.debian.org

Enter 'anonymous' as the user name and leave the
password blank. Click on the 'Quickconnect' button.
You should notice the text at the top of the screen
scrolling when you are connecting to the ftp server.

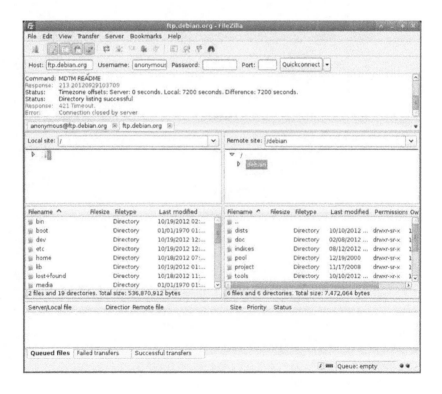

The left side of the screen contains a list of your local files and the right side of the screen displays files that are on the server. Double click on the Debian folder which will display a further list of folders and files. Locate your home directory on the left hand side by double clicking on the home directory and selecting your user name. Right click on the *README* file located on the ftp server and select '*Download*'. You should now be able to locate the downloaded file in your home directory.

Nano
Nano is a very fast text editing program. This is very useful when editing configuration files on your Raspberry Pi.

The example below will start nano.
$ nano

You can also start nano followed by a file name. This has the effect of creating a file when you press enter.

$ nano filename.txt

You are now inside the text editor. You can see a number of options at the bottom of the screen such as ^G Get Help, ^X Exit etc. These options can be invoked by holding down the control key and pressing the letter relating to the option displayed. For example by holding down shift and pressing the '*X*' key will cause nano to exit.

Enter your name into the editor. Hold down the control key and press '*X*'. A message is displayed explaining that you are saving the file.

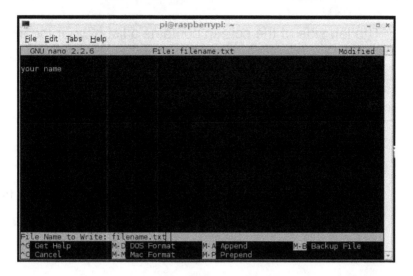

Press 'y' to save the file. Another message is displayed asking you if you want to save the file name as '*filename.txt*'. At this stage you can always save the file using a different name. Press enter to save the file using the existing file name. You have now created a text file called '*filename.txt*'.

CHAPTER 18 - LAMP ON FEDORA REMIX

This chapter will focus on server applications specifically MySql, Apache and PHP. This scenario is commonly referred to as LAMP (**L**inux, **A**pache, **M**ySql, **P**HP). We will start by installing a database which will store data, followed by the installation of Apache which is used to display web pages. PHP will then be installed which will be used to link the data from the database to the web pages.

MySql

Databases are used to store data in many data formats. When you sign up to a web site and you enter your shipping address or home address this information is stored behind the scenes in a relational database. There are many popular databases including MS SQL 2010, Oracle Database, PostgreSQL and MySql to name a few. MySql can also integrate into a web page and display dynamic data such as random products, products from a category or even products in a price range.

Begin by escalating to a root user and entering your password.

```
$ su -
```

Enter the following command.

```
# yum -y install mysql mysql-server
```

MySql will need to be configured so it starts up as soon as the operating system has booted up.

```
# /sbin/chkconfig mysqld on
# /sbin/service mysqld start
```

Next you will need to set the password for MySql.

```
# mysqladmin -u root password 'your-password'
```

To actually connect to mySql enter the following.

```
$ mysql -u root -p
```

You will be prompted to enter your password. After you have done this you will be presented with the mysql> prompt. You have successfully connected to the mySql server. To see the internal databases that are already configured in mySql enter the following mysql commands.

```
mysql> show databases;
```

You should see a list of the following databases.

```
+------------------------------+
| Databases                    |
+------------------------------+
| information_schema           |
| mysql                        |
| performance_schema           |
| test                         |
+------------------------------+
```

Finally type the exit command to quit the mysql client. The mySql server will still continue to run in the background.

```
mysql> exit
```

Apache

Apache is a web server that can be used to display web pages. It can utilise programming languages such as PHP, Ruby etc. These programming languages can be used in a web page to connect to databases and to create dynamic content.

The following steps we will guide you through the process of installing a web server and viewing a basic web page to prove that Apache is working. We will test that PHP has been installed correcting by creating a simple php web page that will display information about apache and php.

Open a terminal window and enter the following as a root user.

```
# yum install httpd
```

When the installation has finished you will need to start the apache web server with the following command.

```
# service httpd start
```

Open the Midori web browser and go to the following local web address.

http://localhost

| Fedora **Test Page** |

This page is used to test the proper operation of the Apache HTTP server after it has been installed. If you can read this page, it means that the web server installed at this site is working properly, but has not yet been configured.

If you are a member of the general public:

The fact that you are seeing this page indicates that the website you just visited is either experiencing problems, or is undergoing routine maintenance.

If you would like to let the administrators of this website know that you've seen this page instead of the page you expected, you should send them e-mail. In general, mail sent to the name "webmaster" and directed to the website's domain should reach the appropriate person.

For example, if you experienced problems while visiting www.example.com, you should send e-mail to "webmaster@example.com".

If you are the website administrator:

You may now add content to the directory /var/www/html/. Note that until you do so, people visiting your website will see this page, and not your content. To prevent this page from ever being used, follow the instructions in the file /etc/httpd/conf.d/welcome.conf.

You are free to use the images below on Apache and Fedora powered HTTP servers. Thanks for using Apache and Fedora!

This screen confirms that the web server is up and running and can display web pages.

PHP

PHP is a general purpose programming language that is perfect for web based applications. It works well with HTML web pages and it lends itself as a conduit between backend databases that can be linked to web pages. This means that content can be pulled from a database can be displayed dynamically. To install PHP follow the instructions below.

```
# yum install php
```

When the installation has finished restart the Apache web server by issuing the following command.

```
# service httpd restart
```

Enter the following command.

```
# nano /var/www/html/test.php
```

Enter the following into the nano editor.

```
<?php
phpinfo();
?>
```

This is php code that will display information confirming that php is functioning as planned.

```
http://localhost/test.php
```

PHP Version 5.3.3-7

System	Linux raspberrypi 3.1.9+ #90 Wed Apr 18 18:23:05 BST 2012 armv6l
Build Date	Feb 10 2012 14:43:43
Server API	Apache 2.0 Handler
Virtual Directory Support	disabled
Configuration File (php.ini) Path	/etc/php5/apache2
Loaded Configuration File	/etc/php5/apache2/php.ini
Scan this dir for additional .ini files	/etc/php5/apache2/conf.d
Additional .ini files parsed	/etc/php5/apache2/conf.d/pdo.ini, /etc/php5/apache2/conf.d/suhosin.ini
PHP API	20090626
PHP Extension	20090626
Zend Extension	220090626
Zend Extension Build	API220090626,NTS
PHP Extension Build	API20090626,NTS
Debug Build	no
Thread Safety	disabled
Zend Memory Manager	enabled
Zend Multibyte Support	disabled
IPv6 Support	enabled
Registered PHP Streams	https, ftps, compress.zlib, compress.bzip2, php, file, glob, data, http, ftp, phar, zip
Registered Stream Socket Transports	tcp, udp, unix, udg, ssl, sslv3, sslv2, tls
Registered Stream Filters	zlib.*, bzip2.*, convert.iconv.*, string.rot13, string.toupper, string.tolower, string.strip_tags, convert.*, consumed, dechunk

The screenshot above is informing you that php has been successfully installed. This page also displays any modules that you have installed such as the MySql module.

CHAPTER 19 - RISC OS

RISC OS is yet another operating system available for the Raspberry Pi. This operating system isn't as pretty as the previous operating systems but it has been designed to allow you the freedom to experiment with speed. It was first release in 1987 by the team that developed the ARM microprocessor. The operating system is small, extremely fast and each program has a very small memory footprint. RISC OS uses a three button mouse when using the desktop. If your mouse does not have three buttons but it does have a scroll wheel then you can always press this down which acts as a middle button.

Download the latest version of RiscOS for the Raspberry Pi below.

https://www.riscosopen.org/content/downloads/other-zipfiles.

Select *Official beta release (ROM image)* from the ROM downloads - Raspberry Pi header. Write this image to your SD card and insert it into your Raspberry Pi.

After you have booted up your Raspberry Pi you will be presented with the desktop.

One thing to mention here is that RISC OS does not have USB Wi-Fi support. If you want to connect to the internet you must use an Ethernet cable or an Ethernet Wi-Fi adapter.

When RISC OS has booted you may notice that networking is not turned off by default.

Move your mouse to the Raspberry Pi icon and left click the mouse button on the icon.

A window will be displayed showing a list of tasks and how much memory is being used. This window functions a little different from what you may be used to. The icon on the top right window will expand the view.

The next icon places the application on the desktop. To reactivate the window, simply double click on the icon. The X on left will close the window. To bring a window to the foreground, click on the bar at the top of the window containing the title.

Click the middle button on the Raspberry Pi icon. This will bring up a RISC OS menu. Move your mouse to the *Info* menu and a window will pop up displaying information about the current version of the operating system. In this case RISC OS 5, version 5.19.

Click on the Raspberry Pi icon again but this time left click your mouse on the configure menu. A configuration window appears containing system configuration icons. To start with we will set up a network connection. Make sure you have an Ethernet cable plugged into your Pi and into a router. Left click your mouse button on the *Network* icon. A window will appear containing three icons. Left click on the *Internet* icon. When another window appears click on the *Enable TCP/IP Protocol Suite* check box. Click on the close button and click on the save button. You will be asked to restart the Raspberry Pi. Click on *Reset* now. When the RISC OS has reloaded double click on the !NetSurf icon.

!NetSurf is a small compact web browser. Notice that the !NetSurf icon appears at the bottom of the screen. Left click on the !NetSurf icon at the bottom to display the browser. In the address bar at the top enter a web address. You should see the web page appear.

You may have noticed that the !NetSurf icon starts with a ! symbol. This symbol in RISC OS is used to indicate that the file is an executable program. Below the !NetSurf icon you have the !StrongEd icon. Again this starts with a ! symbol. Double click on the !StrongEd icon.

The program will appear at the bottom of the desktop. Left click on the icon. !StrongEd is a simple text editor.

To quit an application you will need to click the middle button on the StrongEd icon at the bottom of the desktop and select *quit*.

To shut down the operating system click the middle mouse button on the Raspberry Pi icon and select *shutdown*. You can unplugg the power supply. You can also restart the operating system by clicking on the *Restart* button.

CHAPTER 20 - INSTALLING & REMOVING SOFTWARE

RISC OS has two package managers included called !Store and PackMan.

To install new software double click on the !Store icon.

Left click on the Apps icon.

You will be presented with a list of available applications. Highlight an application name and select the green down arrow icon to download. When the application has downloaded it will open a window. Double click on the icon that starts with a ! symbol. This symbol is referred to a pling.

Double click on the !PackMan icon on the desktop and left click your mouse button on the PackMan icon at the bottom of the desktop. Expand the window so that you can see the descriptions. Highlight the Barrage program and left click your mouse button on the top left icon with the green tick. A window will be displayed giving a summary and the size of the program. Click on the *install* button. After a few seconds the download will complete. Click on the *close* button. Move your mouse to the SD card in the bottom left corner of the desktop and left click your mouse on the SD card icon.

:0

Double click on the *Apps* folder followed by the *Games* folder. Double click on the !Barrage icon. This is the game that you have just downloaded. When you have finished playing the game, press the escape key twice and select *Quit* from the menu.

To remove programs open the PackMan program and highlight the program that you want to remove. Left click the mouse button on the second icon from the left. This contains a box with a red cross next to it. Another window will be displayed with two options. Select the *remove* button and after a few seconds the program will be removed.

CHAPTER 21 - RASPBMC

Raspbmc is a media centre for the Raspberry Pi that is based on the Debian operating system. The great thing about Raspbmc is that you do not need any knowledge of Linux to use it. It has an amazing graphical interface that is intuitive to any user. It is capable of playing movies, audio and displaying images.

Raspbmc will allow you to use Spotify with Raspbmc to stream music and as an optional extra you will be able to control the Raspbmc from a phone or web browser.

The steps required to do this are as follows.

1) Sign up for a premium Spotify account.
2) Write the Raspbmc image to an SD card.
3) Configure Raspmbc to use your wireless network.
4) Download the spotimc script and install.

Additional Steps

Use the analog output to an external amp.

Install the Spotify app on your iPhone for use with Air Play.

Install AirFoil to stream from a computer to Raspbmc.

Connect to the XBMC web server to play control music.

The first thing that you need to do is signup for a Spotify account at www.spotify.com. You can sign up for a free account but in order to get Spotify running with the Raspbmc you will need to use the premium 30 day free trial. This will not cost you anything if you unsubscribe as soon as you have activated the premium account. If you already have a premium account then you are good to go.

Download Raspbmc from www.raspbmc.com and write the image to an SD card. Before you boot up your Raspberry Pi, Raspbmc must have a wired connection to start the installation so make sure an Ethernet cable is connected to your and that this cable is connected to a network point or a router.

CHAPTER 22 - CONFIGURING RASPBMC

When Raspbmc has loaded you will need to configure various settings starting with your language settings.

When the Raspbmc dashboard appears move your mouse to the *programs* menu and select the *Raspbmc Settings* below and click *OK*.

In the *network configuration* menu change the *Network Mode* setting to *Wired* by clicking on the up arrow until it reads *Wireless (WIFI) Network*. Scroll down until you see the menu *WIFI SSID*. Left click the mouse button on this menu item and delete the *raspbmc* entry and enter your wireless network broadcast SSID. Click *Done* when it has finished. Select your WIFI security type. By default WPA/WPA2 is selected and is used by most wireless routers. Next enter your *Wi-Fi key* by clicking on the WIFI KEY menu and click on the *Done* button.

Click on the *Update Now* entry at the bottom of the list Click *OK* to return to the dashboard. Unplug your Ethernet cable and go to the *system menu* and select *System info*.

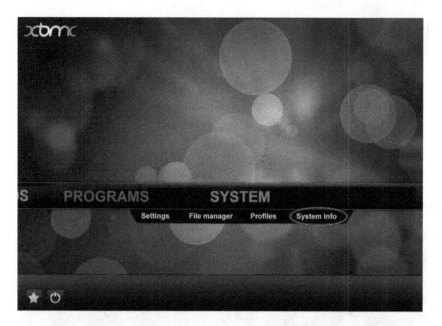

Click on the *Network menu* and check that you have a valid IP address and that the link is connected. Take a note of the IP address as you will need this so that we can connect to it later using a web browser.

CHAPTER 23 - INSTALLING SPOTIFY

SSH into your Raspberry Pi using the login of pi and the password of raspberry and click OK to the security alert. When the following messages is displayed press CTRL-C.

Hi there! You have logged into your Pi for the first time
Allow me to set up your timezone and keyboard settings
Please wait a few seconds...

Enter the following command.

cd /opt/xbmc-bcm/xbmc-bin/share/xbmc/addons

Download the following script by entering the following command.

wget http://www.raspberrypi-tutorials.co.uk/scripts/script.audio.spotimc.zip

Next we need to download the unzip package because it does not exists on Raspbmc. Enter the following.

$ sudo apt-get install unzip

When the package has installed enter the following to unzip the script.

$ sudo unzip script.audio.spotimc.zip

Reboot the raspberry pi for the changes to take effect.

$ sudo shutdown -r 0

Return to the Raspbmc dashboard and select *ad-ons* below the music menu. Click the *OK* button. You will see an entry named *Spotimc.* Click on this and on the next screen click on the *yes* button. Spotimc will update after a few seconds. Go to the music menu and select *ad-ons* and click on the Spotimc menu. A screen will appear asking you to enter you Spotify login details. Enter your Username and Password. You will need to make sure that you have a premium account. Remember that you can always sign up for a premium account and then unsubscribe to get the 30 day free trial.

Check the *Remember me* checkbox and click on the *Login* button. You should be presented with the Spotifmc screen.

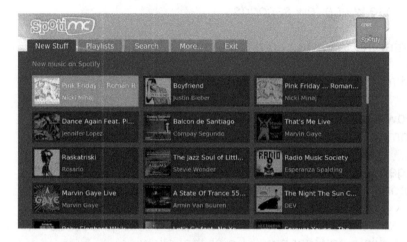

Click on the search button and search for a song. When you have found the song you want simply double click it. The great thing about Spotify is that not only do you have access to millions of songs but it also allows you to create playlists. To learn more about Spotify I suggest you take a look at their web site.

Click *Exit* so that you return to the Raspbmc menu. Next we will set some configuration options. Depending on the set up required you can follow the instructions below.

CHAPTER 24 -SPOTIFY SCENARIOS

Analog

This scenario can be used if you want to use the 3.5mm jack connection on the Raspberry Pi. You can connect to an amp or an audio device that accepts external input. If you want to hear audio using the analog device click on the System->Settings->System->Audio output. Select the up arrow next to the Audio output to select *Analog*.

Air Play

To enable Airplay go to System->Settings->Serivces->AirPlay to allow XBMC to receive AipPlay content. Check the Allow XBMC to receive AirPlay content button. This will allow Spotify on an iPhone to stream the content to the Raspberry Pi.

Webserver

To enable access to XBMC using a browser select System->Settings-Services->Webserver and check the *Allow control of*

XBMC via http button. You should set a username and password for security reasons.

Remote Control

To enable remote access to XBMC using an Android or iPhone application select System->Settings-Remote control and check the *Allow programs on other systems to control XBMC*.

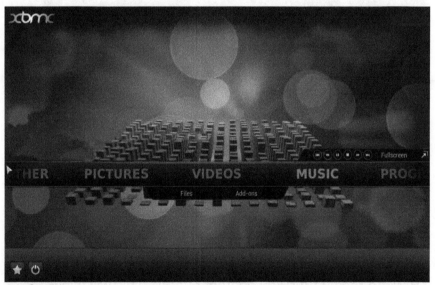

Airfoil

Airfoil is a great utility for allowing your PC to stream music from Spotify to Raspbmc. You can download and install it for free but it is limited to 10 minutes air time unless you purchase it. When you install Airplay it will automatically locate your Raspbmc.

You will need to select Spotify as the source of the audio and select the destination device. In this case it will be XBMC. The diagram below demonstrates a typical set up that shows how to stream from a phone or a PC.

Spotify

Air Foil &
Spotify

CHAPTER 25 - TWEAKING

You can configure most Linux distributions to run faster by allocating more memory to the desktop or processor depending on your needs. Each distribution will provide you with a tool on how to do this but in the event it doesn't you may have to do this manually. Debian Wheezy uses the rasp-config tool to do this which will save you the hassle but you should have an understanding on how this functions.

To do this manually Debian provides you with pre-configured files which are stored in the /boot directory. When you boot Debain or Fedora a file called start.elf is used to partition the memory between the CPU and the GPU. You will need to replace start.elf with the file in the boot directory that best suits your memory needs. For example the file below has the value of 128 within its filename.
arm128_start.elf

The value of 128 is referring to the amount of RAM dedicated to the CPU. The remainder is given to the GPU. To use this memory split you will need to overwrite the start.elf file by using the following commands. Be sure that you are a root user otherwise this operation will deny you from copying the files.

cp /boot/arm128_start.elf /boot/start.elf

You will need to reboot your Raspberry Pi for the memory change to take effect.

If you want to partition the memory so that the CPU has 240MB of RAM use the following.

```
# cp /boot/arm240_start.elf /boot/start.elf
```

Overclocking

You may also find that the desktop can run a little slow especially when using some of the more graphical intense programs. Another option available is to overclock the Raspberry Pi by increasing its speed. The Raspberry Pi uses a file in the boot directory called config.txt. Entries can be added to this file which determines its operating speed. You can increase the CPU and GPU's speed independently of each other and also change the speed at which RAM is accessed. For example by adding the following line will increase the CPU to 800MHz instead of its default speed of 700Mhz.

```
arm_freq=800
```

If you need to increase the speed of the GPU just add the following line. The default speed is set to 240Mhz

```
gpu_freq=280
```

To increase the GPU's 3D rendering hardware capabilities add the following line.

```
v3d_freq=280
```

The default is set to 250MHz. This setting is used to increase gaming performance when using 3D hardware or when some type of 3D rendering is required.

You can also increase the RAM speed from its default of 400MHz to 440MHz by adding the following line.

```
sdram_freq=440
```

PART III
PROGRAMMING

CHAPTER 26 -PYTHON PROGRAMMING

The Raspberry Pi has a host of programming languages and tools that allow you to program the device. Python, C, C++, TinyBasic and assembly are languages that the Raspberry Pi and Linux for that fact can utilise. Each language has its own strengths and weaknesses depending on your view.

If Python isn't already installed or you can use apt-get, Synaptic or the yum command to install it from the prompt.

The great thing about Python is that you can use a program called IDLE. IDLE is an integrated development environment (IDE) for Python which will display instant results as you press enter on each line. This will allow rapid software development and will also highlight any obvious mistakes.
You can start IDLE by moving your mouse to the Programming menu and select IDLE3.
Press enter.

You will notice that the following symbols appear >>>. This is an indication to the user that IDLE is ready to accept Python commands.

Enter the following lines below.

>>> **x = 10**

>>> **y = 11**

Remember that you only need to enter the lines in bold and not the >>> symbols.

x and y are variables and are used to store values. These values can be names, letters, numbers or even a collection of space aliens. x stores the value of 10 and y stores the value of 11.

Enter the following.

>>> print (x)

10

>>>

>>> print (y)

11

When you press enter after you first *print* command it will display the value stored in x. In this case the value is 10. y contains the value 11 as shown above.

Now enter the following.

>>> print(x+y)
21

The above print command is displaying the result of x added to y. The result is 21. You can also use the - symbol to subtract a value, the * symbol to multiple and the / symbol to divide.

Enter the following examples below.

>>> print (y-x)
1
>>> print (x*y)
110
>>> print (y/x)

You can also assign the result of other variables to new variables. For example enter the following line.

```
>>> result = x + y
>>> print (result)
21
```

The *result* variable has stored the result of x + y. Naming this variable *result* is easier to understand than naming it z. A more realistic program might look like this.

```
>>> your_age = 17
>>> marks_age = 15
>>> combined_age = your_age + marks_age
>>> print (combined_age)
32
```

Up until now you have just seen very short programs. As good as IDLE is it isn't great for writing large programs. Later you will understand how to use an IDE to create programs which will give you greater flexibility when programming.

Before you can create a program you will first need to understand the Python syntax and keywords. Below you will be able to find a quick overview of keywords and examples. If you can't understand any of the syntax below do not worry as this part of the book will be aimed at teaching you how to program. We will start with comments.

Comments are used as notes for the programmer and are ignored by the program. To create a comment you will use the # symbol. The line of code below is a comment.

```
# This is my raspberry pi program and this is a comment
```

Variables

Variables are to store values such as numbers, names, colours, groups of colours and just about anything that can be thought of.

```
score = 610
myName = "Alison"
x_location = 10
```

if.

The *if* statement is used when a decision is required. For example if you own an Xbox 360 and a PS4 then you can make a decision on which game console you would like to play. Let's assume that you pick a random computer game and that you need to know which game console the game can be played on. You read the title of the game and it informs you that it can only be used on a PS4. So the program might look like this.

```
game_type = PS4
if game_type == PS4:
        #this can only be played on a PS4
```

Strings

Strings can be used to store an array of characters. For example the follow snippet of code creates a variable called footballTeam which assigns the string "Liverpool" to the variable. Anything that appears between the " " is a string.

```
footballTeam="Liverpool"
```

print

The print statement is used to print variables or strings to the screen.

```
print("This is my string")

footballTeam = "Liverpool"
print(footballTeam)
```

The output above will first display, 'This is my string' followed by 'Liverpool' on the next line.

Concatenation

Concatenation allows you to add a series of string and numbers together. For example using the example above we can simplify the above code.

```
footballTeam="Millwall"
print("My favourite football team is " + footballTeam
```

The output will be 'My favourite football team is Millwall'.

Functions

A function is used to keep your code clean, prevents you from re-entering the same code and it allows you to change the function in once place and your code throughout will automatically update. Note that the code below myFunction must be indented.

```
def myFunction():
        print("I am a function")

#the instruction below will call myFunction
myFunction()
myFunction()
myFunction()
```

The output will display the following

I am a function

I am a function

I am a function

Notice that it is repeated 3 times. This is because we have called myFunction three times. If the print statement inside the myFunction was changed to

```
def myFunction():
        print("I am programming python")

myFunction()
myFunction()
```

The output will be

I am programming python

I am programming python

Loop

A loop in programming is used when you need the program to repeat a repetitive task. Using the example above we can reduce the code even further by creating a loop.

```
def myFunction():
```

```
print("I am programming python")

for x in range(3):
        myFunction()
```

The above code sample will produce the same output as the
previous example but this example now uses a loop. The *for*
loop is used to call myFunction a specified number of times.

Remember don't worry too much if you found the above
examples confusing. We will start from the very beginning
and build up your knowledge of Python. One of the best ways
to learn programming is to create games. Games are fun and
will allow you to see pleasing graphical representations of your
program. We will also use PyGame with Python to produce a
simple game. PyGame will be used because it will help us to
quickly create a game while using the Python language.
Python and PyGame make an ideal combination for creating
computer games and programs. It has the ability to rapidly
produce amazingly fast computer games which will work on
many computer platforms.

Game creators and software developers will often use words
or sentences that at first seem complex but in reality, when
you break them down, it really isn't that hard to understand. I
will introduce you to these words and their meanings, as and
when you need them. I will also introduce keywords when we
need them as not to bore you with the details before we even
start. It is always best to learn by example rather than just
reading about programming. Unless you actually create any
games, you will never fully understand the issues you are
likely to come up against when programming.

The first few chapters in this book have deliberately been kept
short. I have done this so that the reader does not get bogged
down with details before they have even had a chance to type
a line of program code towards creating their game.

I will also run through most of the common errors in programming because you will learn a lot more from your errors than just copying program code. Looking for errors in your program will change your way of thinking when you start to write programs. You will prevent yourself from making the same mistakes by actually making the mistakes. Making programming mistakes is a good thing, providing you learn from it and change the error before you release your program. You will also find yourself thinking through problems logically and in a sequential order. You will find that game programming is built upon lots of events happening simultaneously, but in reality it is performing one step at a time. It just appears this way because so much is happening so quickly.

CHAPTER 27 - HOW A COMPUTER GAME IS CREATED

Before you create a computer program, it is always a good idea to design and write down a plan of the game. This is referred to as a "***Game Design Document***". In your game design document you should describe what the game does, how the player wins the game how the player loses the game and how the player will control his or her characters. You should include as many details as you can think of but remember that the design needs to be flexible. The reason for this is that you might want to include additional levels if a user gains over 1000 points. You might, at a later stage decide that you want to include a 2 player option. If this is the case, you will need to change your game design.
You should always use diagrams and pictures in your game design document as this is a great way to easily show how the game will look without going into detail.

Things to keep in mind while developing a computer game are
- Your target audience
- Which device is this going to be played on?
- How many players are there going to be in your game?
- Is the game going to be played online with others?
- Do we need to store any user information?

Your target audience
Think about who the game is for. If it is going to be for young children, then you might want to use images that are suitable for children. If the game is for your Grandma, then she might not want to see a fast paced motorbike game.

Which device is this going to be played on?

You need to decide from the beginning which device this game will be played on. Will it be a phone, a laptop, a Raspberry Pi or a tablet? If the game is going to be used on a phone, then you have to be aware that the screen is much smaller on a phone that it is your Raspberry Pi. In this book we will only be targeting the Raspberry Pi.

How many players are going to be in your game?

If the game is going to be a 2 player game, then you need to use 2 scores, 2 sets of lives or energy and a way of controlling each character.

Is the game going to be played online with others?

Things will get a little more complex if you are going to create an online game. The reason for this is that you need to manage the way in which data is sent to and from devices.

Do we need to store any user information?

You might want to store the user high score information along with their name or if you are creating an adventure game, you might want to store that last place the user last saved the game.

Now that you have an idea of the first step, you need to understand what is needed to start creating a game. In order to create a computer game, you have to create a list of instructions that the computer can understand. This list is called your program. The program which contains your list of instructions is fed to something called the 'Python interpreter'. The interpreter's job is to translate these instructions so that your computer can display your game.

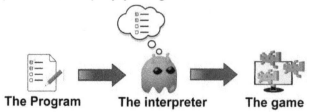

The Program   The interpreter   The game

In the screenshot above, you can see that the program is being fed into the interpreter, which will translate the instructions and display the game on your screen.

CHAPTER 28 - SO WHAT IS PYTHON?

In order to create a computer game, you will need to instruct the computer on what and how to do it. Before you can instruct the computer on how to do this, you must first learn a language that both you and the computer can understand. This language is called Python. Python is an easy language to learn which will help you solve the problems faced by many game developers working in the industry today.

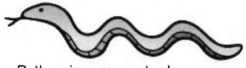

Python is a computer language

Python also contains many pre written programs or source code which you can use for free. This will save you from creating a program that already exists. It will also allow you to change the way these programs are created in case you don't like the way it functions. It is about time I showed you what the Python language looks like.

```
name = "Alison Watson"
print("hello world")
answer = 2 + 2
print("hello world")
```

If you have never seen a computer program before, you should be able understand some of the program as it should be familiar to things you do in your ever day life.
It is not important to understand the above program yet as I will take you through programs later in the following chapters. All you need to understand for now is that Python is a computer language that will help us create games.

CHAPTER 29 - WHAT IS PYGAME?

PyGame is a set of programs that we can use when creating our games. These programs contain features that have already been created for us that we can utilise in our games. For example, if we want to draw a rectangle or a circle, then this already exists in Pygame. All we need to do is use it. Rather than instructing our program on how a rectangle is created, we can concentrate on how to use it.

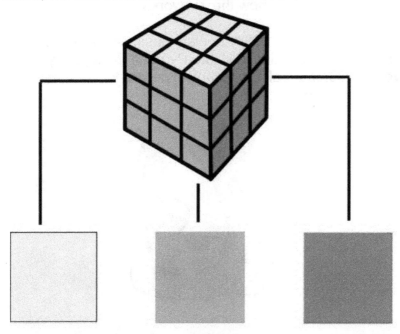

The rectangles have already been created for us. We just need to use them.

If you are confused you can think of it like this. You know how to use your TV or iPod but you don't need to know how it was assembled. All you want to know is that when you turn it on and play music or change the channel, it will do just that.

Changing the TV channel does not require you to understand how the TV works.

Pygame also has the ability to play music and sound effects in your game. This is also built into Pygame, so again, you don't have to understand all the technical details to use these features.

CHAPTER 30 - INSTALLING PYGAME

Installing Pygame is a simple process using the console. First you need to start your desktop environment if you haven't already done so. This is done by typing the following command after you have logged into your Raspberry Pi.

```
$ startx
```

Your Raspberry Pi desktop will appear.
Open a terminal and enter the following command to install Pygame.

```
$ sudo apt-get install python-pygame
```

When prompted to continue with the installation, press Y. You will be presented with information regarding the Pygame installation which will appear similar to that below, although the output here has been shortened.

```
...
Processing triggers for python-central ...
Setting up python-pygame () ...
Processing triggers for python-central ...
...
```

Assuming that no errors occurred during the installation, you will have Pygame installed.

If you are using Fedora Remix then you can use the following.

```
su -
yum install pygame
```

CHAPTER 31 - THE GEANY IDE

In order to create a game, we are going to need something to type our program into. These programs are called Integrated Development Environments. These programs will keep your files organised and will allow us to quickly run and test our game.

REMEMBER: A game can consist of not only our program code but also music files, graphic files and many other resources.

There are a number of development environments including SPE, Geany, Eclipse, PyDev and so on. We will concentrate on using the Geany IDE. Install the Geany IDE for your operating system. If you are using Debian then enter the following to install it.

```
$ sudo apt-get install geany
```

If you are using Fedora Remix then escalate to a root user and enter the following.

```
# yum install geany
```

For any other operating systems follow the link below.

http://www.geany.org/Download/ThirdPartyPackages

It is time to get your hands dirty. We will open Geany and create a blank file.   This will allow us to enter some program code that will test if Pygame is installed. Before we start using Geany we will run through an overview of what Geany looks like and how it can help us. The screenshots below have been taken on a Debian operating system but the process if the same.
Click your left mouse button on the Geany icon.

Next, move your mouse pointer over to the menu that says, **Programming**.

Left click the mouse button on the **Geany** menu item.   After a few seconds, Geany will open.

At the top of Geany, you will find the drop down menus that are needed to perform certain actions. For example, if you click on the **File menu,** it will display a menu containing a list of file options.

The toolbar contains a list of shortcuts or commonly used options that we will use while programming. The left panel in Geany is the file area. This will allow us quick and easy access to our files. Just to the right of this, above the programming area, you will see a tab labelled, "*untitled*". This is the name of the file name. The reason the file name is called "*untitled*", is because we haven't named the file yet. The programming area is where we will write our program. Below this you will see an area that contains status, compiler and messages tabs. This area is used to inform us of any error messages or informational messages that Geany thinks we should know about.

Begin by creating a new empty file. Left click your mouse button on icon below, circled in red. This is the *'create a new file'* icon.

Enter the following line of code into your programming area.

```
import pygame
print(pygame.version.ver)
```

This program above should be entered directly into the programming area within Geany. This short program will output which version of Pygame that you currently have installed.

Now we need to save the file. We will save the file name as, *'PygameTest.py'*. Go to the menu called, *'File'* and then left click your mouse button on *'Save As'* menu item. The image below will show you how to save the file.

When you have clicked on the *'Save As'* menu item, you will be presented with a window asking you for a name. Before we save this file, we need to create a folder to hold all our files. We are going to organise our files in a Folder called Projects. You can think of this as storing all your personal paperwork in a draw labelled **Projects**.

The image below demonstrates how a folder is used.

OurProgramFile.py

Projects
Folder

In the image above, the program called 'OurProgramFile.py' is stored in a folder called '*Projects*'.

To create the folder click on the button that is labelled, '*Create Folder*'.

Type in the name of a folder, which in this case is going to be '*Projects*' and press enter.

Now that the folder has been created, we need to name the file. Left click your mouse button on the top text field, next to the Name label and enter, '*PygameTest.py.* Left* click your mouse button on '*Save*'.

We are now ready to test our program. To execute or run your program, left click your mouse button on the icon that looks like some mechanical cogs.

This icon is used to run our program. If all goes well, you will be presented with the following output.

```
geany_run_script.sh                           _  □  ×
1.9.1release


-------------------
(program exited with code: 0)
Press return to continue
```

I have version 1.9.1 of Pygame installed but your version may report something different.

Go ahead and close your program by clicking on the X in the top right corner of the black terminal window.

CHAPTER 32 - THE GAME DESIGN DOCUMENT

The purpose of a game design document is so that you or anyone else reading the document can understand how the game is played and the resources that it uses. A game design document will keep us focused on how the final game should look. The document is sometimes referred to as a 'Living Document', because it is constantly changing and may be modified with new ideas as you progress. The document can contain text, diagrams, concept art work, images and any type of media that is relevant to the game.

A brief list of what might appear in your game design document is:

- Project or game title
- The date that this document was produced
- A list of people involved in the development of the game
- The version number of this document and the version number of the game it relates to
- Design History
- Game overview
- Game features
- Game characters
- Level design
- Gameplay
- Artwork
- Sound and Music
- Game controls
- The user interface of HUD

This list can be expanded with any other relevant information that is required to fit your game. You should also include when the player has completed the game and when they have lost the game.

Note: Not every game will contain the entire list above. You may find that some options above don't apply to your game.

Based on the game that we are going to write in the next chapter, we will create a basic game design document. It will look something like this.

Treasure Quest

Document version: 1.0
28/06/2012

Programming: Your Name
Graphics : Your Name
Music & sound effects: None

Design History

Version 1.0. At the moment this is not relevant because this is the first version of the game design document. Later as you tweak the game, this section will become more relevant.

Overview

The game is set on a remote island in the Caribbean. The objective of this game is to control the player character and to locate the buried treasure.

Gameplay

This game will be in the style of an arcade game in which the player will run around the island looking for the buried treasure. The player will control the pirate and the treasure will be a stationary image. The player will win the game as soon as the player character reaches the treasure at which point the game will quit. The game can also be terminated if the user presses the red X on the window.

Game features
One level
One player
A map of an island
The treasure
The player character

Game characters
The player character will be a pirate.
The treasure will be a treasure chest containing gold coins.
Level design
The design below uses a single screen with a single level. If the player reaches the treasure, the player wins and the game is over. There is no way for the player to lose.

Artwork

 The player

 The treasure

Sound and Music
None
Game controls
The game will be controlled by the user using the keyboard.
The UP, DOWN, LEFT and RIGHT arrow keys will be used to
move the player character around the screen.
User Interface / HUD
None. This will normally display user lives, points, score and
so on.

Next we should write out the program using plain English but
we need to break it down to into logical steps. Normally you
would create another document containing these details as
this can become very large but for now, we will just add a new
heading to the game design document. This heading will be
called, 'How to play".
You can think of this as a simple step by step guide on how
the game is going to work.

How to play
While the game is running
        If the player clicks on the red X in the window, the
game will end
        Draw the island background
        Move the player
        Draw the player
        Draw the treasure
        If the player reaches the treasure, the player wins and
the game will end

Take a minute to go through each step. Each step will represent part of the program that we are going to program. Notice that the lines after, 'While the game is running', are indented. This is because these lines occur within a game loop. A game loop is used to update everything in a game until the game ends. Game loops will be explored further later but for now just remember that a game is also running even if a player isn't playing the game.

CHAPTER 33 - YOUR FIRST PYGAME PROGRAM

Now that you understand how the game will work and how it will look, we can press ahead and start programming our basic game. Login into your Raspberry Pi desktop and start Geany. From your terminal prompt type the following to start your desktop.

```
$ startx
```

In case you can't remember how to open Geany, just go into the 'Programming' menu item and left click your mouse button on the 'Geany' menu icon.
Now that Geany is open, you will need to create an empty file in the 'Projects' folder that you created earlier. Click on the new document icon to create an empty file.

We will add a few lines at a time explaining what each line does as we progress. This will progress in a simple game.

Enter the following lines into the empty file.

```
import pygame
import sys
pygame.init()
```

The first line will import all the built in programs that are required for pygame. Remember that instead of creating a rectangle from scratch, we will just use the rectangle that Pygame supplies. The next line, '*import sys*' is used for when we want to use the built in exit function later in our game. If we didn't import sys then we would not be able to close our game window down easily. Below this is, pygame.init(). This line does a lot of work behind the scenes and sets up Pygame so we can start using it. pygame.init() is a something that is called a function. A function can be thought of a piece of code that you can call upon to do some work. More on functions will be explained later.

Enter the following lines below the lines you have entered above

```
# the width and height of the screen
(screen_width, screen_height) = (400, 300)
```

At the start of this line, you will notice a '#' symbol. These symbols are called comments and they are not used by our program. They are simply ignored by our program. They are there as notes to the programmer so that we can inform the reader what is happening. It is also a reminder for ourselves when we revisit this game in a few months' time but have forgotten how we did something.

The screen_width and screen_height are called variables and they are used to store values. In this case the width of the screen is 400 and the height is 300.

(screen_width, screen_height) = (400, 300)

Enter the following lines into your program.

```
#set up the screen size and mode and store the returned
#screen data into the screen variable
screen = pygame.display.set_mode((screen_width,
screen_height))
```

The above lines start with a comment that is ignored by your
program. The line that actually does something is the last line.
This line sets up the screen so we can start using it. You will
notice that the screen_width and screen_height variables
appear inside the display.set_mode function.
Remember that a function can be thought of a piece of code
that you can call upon to do some work. For example, you
might not want to cut the grass in your garden. In that case
you can call upon a gardener to do the work. You might even
want him to tell you when he has finished. If you ask him to let
you know when he has finished, then he is returning some
information to you. This is what is happening in the above line
of code. We are asking the pygame.display.set_mode
function to create a screen that is 400 in width and 300 in
height.

Remember that we have assigned screen_width the value of
400 and the screen_height the value of 300.

Your program should look this so far.

```
import pygame
import sys

pygame.init()
# the width and height of the screen
(screen_width, screen_height) = (400, 300)

#set up the screen size and mode and store the returned
#screen data into the screen variable
screen = pygame.display.set_mode((screen_width,
screen_height))
```

The information returned from the pygame.display.set_modefunction is stored in something called a variable. I haven't explained clearly what a variable is yet but you have already been using them. You can think of a variable as something that will store information. This information can be your age, your name, a screen or an image. It is always a good idea to create variables with meaningful names.

Remember: A variable can store numbers, letters, words, music or even pirates.

You can think of it as a box that we can put things in such as homework, football shoes, skipping ropes or peoples name.

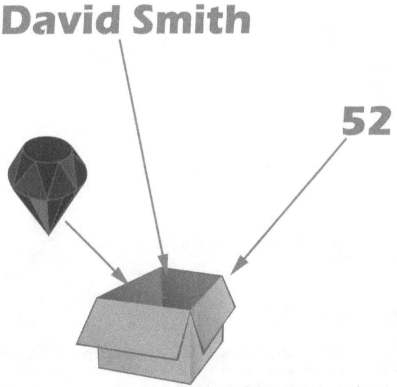

The box represents the variable and the name, number and the diamonds can be stored inside variables.

Variables are not only for storing things in. We can also take out whatever we put in there.

Now that you are clear on what a variable is and how it can be used to store and retrieve information from them, we can move on.

Enter the following lines.

```
#used to determine if the game is running
game_is_running = True
```

This above line will be used to indicate that the game is running. We are assigning the value of True to game_is_running. If the value was False, then the game would not be running.

You program should now look like this.

```
import pygame
import sys

init.pygame()

#the width and height of the screen
(screen_width, screen_height) = (400, 300)

#set up the screen size and mode and store the returned
#screen data into screen
screen = pygame.display.set_mode((screen_width,
screen_height))

#used to determine if the game is running
game_is_running = True
```

This is what our program does so far. It imports everything we need to use pygame successfully. It then sets up pygame by calling the function init.pygame().

We then set up the screen width and the height by storing these values in the variables, screen_width and screen_height. We created our screen by passing in the screen_width and screen_height to the function pygame.display.set_mode, which will create our screen for us and return it to our variable called screen.

A variable called game_is_running is created, which has the value of '*True*'. This will be used to let the program know that the game is being played.

The above program sets up everything we need so we can move on to the core of our game.

Enter the following lines below the existing program.

```
#while the game is still running
while game_is_running:
```

This line start with a python keyword called while. While can be thought of as while something is happening or while the car engine is running. In our case, while game_is_running. As the game_is_running variable is true, it is the same as saying while true. As long as the variable, game_is_running remains '*True*', the game will continue. Notice that at the end of this variable is a ':' symbol. This means that we are going to create a loop. A loop in this case is a while loop, which we stated at the beginning of the line.

Go ahead and enter the next line but before you start the line, press the tab key so that the following lines are indented. This indenting indicates to our program that we want to carry out the following actions within a loop.

```
#for every event that happens in our game
for event in pygame.event.get():
```

Before I explain what the above line does, let's check how the program should look like.

```
import pygame
import sys

pygame.init()

#the width and height of the screen
(screen_width, screen_height) = (400, 300)

#set up the screen size and mode and store the returned
#screen data into screen
screen = pygame.display.set_mode((screen_width,
screen_height))

#used to determine if the game is running
game_is_running = True

#while the game is still running
while game_is_running:

    #for every event that happens in our game
    for event in pygame.event.get():
```

This line reads that for every event, in pygame events. It may sound confusing but it isn't. Keep reading and all will become a little clearer. Starting at the beginning of this line

```
    for event in pygame.event.get():
```

'*For*' is just another type of loop. A for loop will loop though a list until there are no more items. For example, the image below has three items on the shopping list.

If we were to write this out in a 'for loop', it would look like this.

For every_item in shopping_list
  Display item name

When all the items in the shopping list have been displayed
the loop will finish.

But what is an event? An event is something that alerts you.
Some alerts you are interested in such as setting your alarm
clock and 7:00am. At 7:00am your alarm clock will buzz and
will wake you up. Other events, such as the sandwich delivery
truck that will be arriving in 10 minutes, might not be of any
concern to you because you have already eaten.
The variable that stores these event types is the 'event'
variable after. For example, using the image below, you can
see that the X key has been pressed and is stored in the event
type variable.

for event in pygame.event.get():

You only need to look for event types that you are interested.
If you are only interested in knowing if the user pressed the Y
key, then the mouse moving is of no interest to you. Pay
attention to the ':' symbol at the end of this line.

Next, enter the following line which will look for the event type
of QUIT. This event type will exit the game. You will need to
indent the code again by pressing the tab key.

```
#if the event is a quit event then exit
if event.type == pygame.QUIT:
    exit()
```

The program so far is listed below.

```
import pygame
import sys

pygame.init()

#the width and height of the screen
(screen_width, screen_height) = (400, 300)

#set up the screen size and mode and store the returned
#screen data into screen
screen = pygame.display.set_mode((screen_width,
screen_height))

#used to determine if the game is running
game_is_running = True
```

```
#while the game is still running
while game_is_running:

    #for every event that happens in our game
    for event in pygame.event.get():

        #if the event is a quit event then exit
        if event.type == pygame.QUIT:
            exit()
```

Notice how the tab is used to indent the code. The line above uses the '*if*' keyword. If the user presses their left mouse button on the red X to close the window, then the event type will be '*pygame.QUIT*'. If the event type is equal to '*pygame.QUIT*', which it is if the user closed the window, the program will exit.

Enter the following lines which will update our display with any changes we have made.

```
#draw our temporary screen to the actual screen
pygame.display.update()
```

Now you are ready to see the final result. Your completed program should look like this.

```
import pygame
import sys

pygame.init()

#the width and height of the screen
(screen_width, screen_height) = (400, 300)

#set up the screen size and mode and store the returned
#screen data into screen
screen = pygame.display.set_mode((screen_width,
screen_height))
```

```
#used to determine if the game is running
game_is_running = True

#while the game is still running
while game_is_running:

    #for every event that happens in our game
    for event in pygame.event.get():

        #if the event is a quit event then exit
        if event.type == pygame.QUIT:
            exit()

    #draw our temporary screen to the actual screen
    pygame.display.update()
```

To run the program, just press your left mouse the compile icon which looks like the mechanical cogs.

When you run the program you should see a black game window. The 'while' loop is now running and the *'for event'* is receiving all the events that this window generates. This could be anything from the mouse moving across the screen to the window being closed. Click on the red X in the top right hand corner of the game window. When you do this, a pygame.quit event.type is generated. The line below compares the event type with the pygame.QUIT event. This event type matches pygame.QUIT, so the program jumps to the next line which informs our game to exit.

```
if event.type == pygame.QUIT:
    exit()
```

File name: TheWindow.py

CHAPTER 34 - ADDING BACKGROUND IMAGES

Continuing from where we left off in the last chapter, enter the following line after you have set up the screen. This line will load the island image into the variable called, background.

```
screen = pygame.display.set_mode((screen_width,
screen_height))

#load the background image
background = pygame.image.load("background.png")
```

In order for this to work, you must have an image file called, 'background.png' in the current directory.

You program should now look like this.

```
import pygame
import sys

init.pygame()

#the width and height of the screen
(screen_width, screen_height) = (400, 300)

#set up the screen size and mode and store the returned
#screen data into screen
screen = pygame.display.set_mode((screen_width,
screen_height))

#load the background image
background = pygame.image.load("background.png")

#used to determine if the game is running
```

```
game_is_running = True
```

Just to recap. Our program imports everything we need to use pygame successfully and initialises pygame so that it is ready to use. The screen width and height is assigned to the appropriate variables. We create the screen which will allow us to draw on it. The background is loaded and stored in the background variable. We are using the game_is_running variable to indicate if the game is running.
The program so far is listed below.

```python
import pygame
import sys

pygame.init()

#the width and height of the screen
(screen_width, screen_height) = (400, 300)

#set up the screen size and mode and store the returned
#screen data into screen
screen = pygame.display.set_mode((screen_width,
screen_height))

#load the background image
background = pygame.image.load("background.png")

#used to determine if the game is running
game_is_running = True

#while the game is still running
while game_is_running:

    #for every event that happens in our game
    for event in pygame.event.get():

        #if the event is a quit event then exit
        if event.type == pygame.QUIT:
            exit()
```

Enter the following lines which will display the background on the screen and update the display.

```
#draw the background at screen location 0,0
screen.blit(background, (0,0))

#draw our temporary screen to the actual screen
pygame.display.update()
```

The key thing to note in the above code is the, 'screen.blit'. Blit or blitting means to copy from one image variable to the screen. In our case it will copy our background image to our screen. The (0,0) represents the screen X and Y position. The first 0 represents the X coordinate and the next 0 is Y coordinate. As we have entered (0,0), this is positioning our image in the top left corner of the screen.

Now you are ready to see the final result. Your completed program should look like this.

```
import pygame
import sys

pygame.init()

#the width and height of the screen
(screen_width, screen_height) = (400, 300)

#set up the screen size and mode and store the returned
#screen data into screen
screen = pygame.display.set_mode((screen_width,
screen_height))

#load the background image
background = pygame.image.load("background.png")

#used to determine if the game is running
game_is_running = True
```

```
#while the game is still running
while game_is_running:

    #for every event that happens in our game
    for event in pygame.event.get():

        #if the event is a quit event then exit
        if event.type == pygame.QUIT:
            exit()

    #draw the background at screen location 0,0
    screen.blit(background, (0,0))

    #draw our temporary screen to the actual screen
    pygame.display.update()
```

Run the program.

The follow window is displayed containing the island background image.

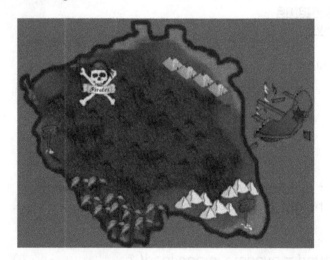

At the start of this book I said that it is a good thing to make mistakes in programming because you will learn a lot more than just copying code. We are going to go ahead and make a mistake so that we can see which error message is displayed.

Change the line that reads

```
#load the background image
background = pygame.image.load("background.png")
```

to the following.

```
#load the background image
background = pygame.image.load("abc.png")
```

The file name called 'abc.png' does not exist and therefore the image will not be able to load. Go ahead and run the program again. You should see the window appear and then close again. The following error message is displayed.

```
Traceback (most recent call last):
  File "ThePlayer.py", line 14, in <module>
    background = pygame.image.load("abc.png")
      pygame.error: Couldn't open abc.png
```

The program ran until it reached line 14 and then an error occurred. This is confirmed by the error message displaying the actual line of code that caused the problem. Below this line it is reporting that the file could not open the file.
This is an error that still occurs with all programmers and typos are normally to blame. The other problem could be that the file just does not exist in that location. For example, if you have a folder called 'images' which contains all your images used on your game but then you tell your program to look for an image file in the current directory, then it will not find it. Instead, you would have to create a line that reads.

```
#load the background image
background = pygame.image.load("images/background.png")
```

Go ahead and change the background name back to its original file name.

```
#load the background image
```

```
background = pygame.image.load("background.png")
```

File name: TheBackground.py

CHAPTER 35 - ADDING THE PLAYER

In this chapter we are going to add the player. The player will appear near the ship on the island. Enter the following lines to create the player. These lines should be entered below the background image. To clarify, the line you should be entering will be highlighted in yellow.

```
#load the background image
background = pygame.image.load("background.png")

#the player
player = pygame.image.load("player_pirate.png")
```

Now that the player image exists in the player variable, we can now go ahead and blit the image to the screen.

```
#draw the background at screen location 0,0
screen.blit(background, (0,0))

#draw the player
screen.blit(player, (300, screen_height / 2))
```

We are now blitting or drawing the image to the screen. The blit function accepts an X and Y location. For the X location, we used 300 but for the Y location we applied some simple mathematics. We take the screen_height value, which is 300 and we divide it by 2. This gives us the Y location 150.
Your program should now look like the following program.

```
import pygame
import sys

pygame.init()

#the width and height of the screen
```

```
(screen_width, screen_height) = (400, 300)

#set up the screen size and mode and store the returned
#screen data into screen
screen = pygame.display.set_mode((screen_width,
screen_height))

#load the background image
background = pygame.image.load("background.png")

#the player
player = pygame.image.load("player_pirate.png")

#used to determine if the game is running
game_is_running = True

#while the game is still running
while game_is_running:

    #for every event that happens in our game
    for event in pygame.event.get():

        #if the event is a quit event then exit
        if event.type == pygame.QUIT:
            exit()

    #draw the background at screen location 0,0
    screen.blit(background, (0,0))

    #draw the player
    screen.blit(player, (300, screen_height / 2))

    #draw our temporary screen to the actual screen
    pygame.display.update()
```

Run the program and examine where the player character
appears.

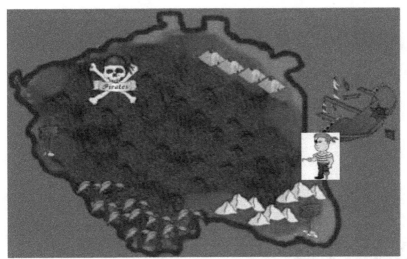

The top left corner of the player image is 300 in X, and 150 in Y. We have used these X and Y values but as yet, I haven't explained exactly what they are. These values are known as screen pixels.

Your computer screen is made up of tiny little squares, each containing a colour. If you could zoom in on your monitor, you would notice these tiny squares called pixels. A pixel is just one square on a screen but your screen has lots of pixels so that it can create images.

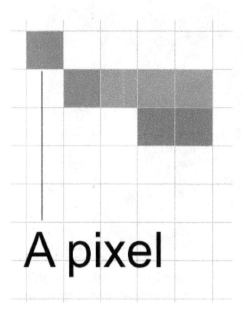

A pixel

When we zoom away from the monitor, we can no longer see the pixels but we do see an entire image made of up of colourful pixels.

The image below has been zoomed in which makes the image looked pixelated or blocky. You will see the different coloured pixels that are used to make up the image.

Now take a look at the same image but this time the image is not zoomed in and is at its original size.

You can no longer see the pixels that make up this image. Now you know what a pixel is, let's move on to the diagram below. The diagram below explains pixel positioning. The image below is showing you that the starting position of the rectangle is 300 pixels from the left of the window in the X coordinate and the 300 pixels in Y coordinate from the top of the window.

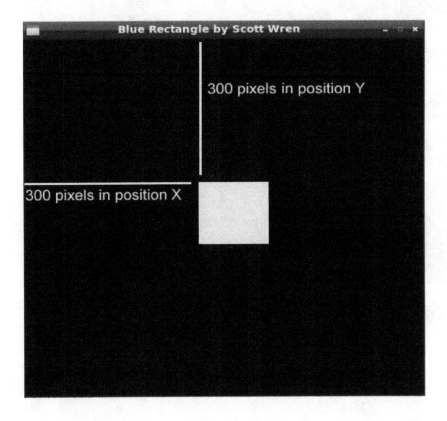

When the objects are moved from the top of the screen towards the bottom, the Y value will increase. In the image above, you can see that we have moved the yellow rectangle down the screen, 300 pixels. The X position have been moved 300 pixels to the right, which increases it value. In the image above, the X value is 300 pixels. When we use this method of positioning objects on the screen, it will be represented as 300, 300. The X position is always first.
If the rectangle was to be placed at X 100 and Y 300, then it would appear in the window as displayed in the image below.

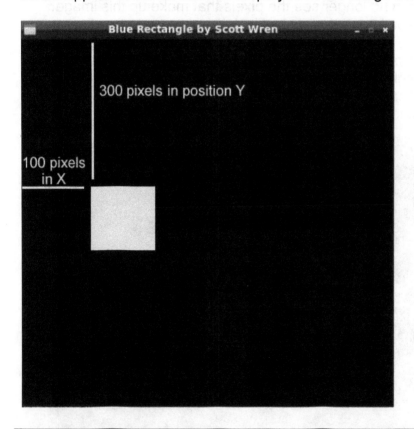

File name: TheTreasure.py

CHAPTER 36 - ADDING THE TREASURE

The island background is now being displayed in our window and the player is in position on the island. We now need to add the treasure by adding the following highlighted code.

```python
import pygame
import sys

pygame.init()

#the width and height of the screen
(screen_width, screen_height) = (400, 300)

#set up the screen size and mode and store the returned
#screen data into screen
screen = pygame.display.set_mode((screen_width,
screen_height))

#load the background image
background = pygame.image.load("background.png")

#the player
player = pygame.image.load("player_pirate.png")

#the treasure
treasure = pygame.image.load("treasure.png")

#used to determine if the game is running
game_is_running = True

#while the game is still running
while game_is_running:

    #for every event that happens in our game
    for event in pygame.event.get():

        #if the event is a quit event then exit
        if event.type == pygame.QUIT:
```

```
        exit()

#draw the background at screen location 0,0
screen.blit(background, (0,0))

#draw the player
screen.blit(player, (280, 210))

#draw the treasure
screen.blit(treasure, (160, 20))

#draw our temporary screen to the actual screen
pygame.display.update()
```

You will notice that we are no longer using simple math to position the player. This is because every time the player needs to be drawn on the screen, Python would have to calculate its position. It is far more efficient to give it a constant number so that Python does not have to perform unnecessary calculations.

Go ahead a run your program. You should see the player and the treasure in position.

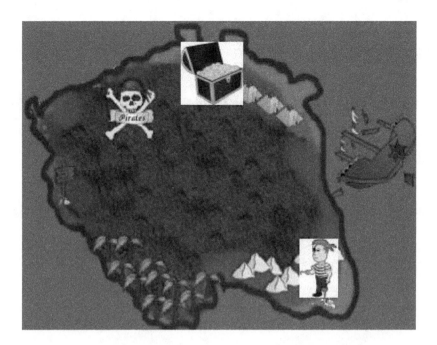

The player image and the treasure image are surrounded by a white block of colour. This is because images are like paintings on a wall. They are either square or rectangle. We can however use a trick to remove this white block of colour and therefore giving the appearance of an irregular image or shape.

Go ahead and make the changes that are highlighted to your program.

```
import pygame
import sys

pygame.init()

#the width and height of the screen
(screen_width, screen_height) = (400, 300)

#set up the screen size and mode and store the returned
#screen data into screen
```

```python
screen = pygame.display.set_mode((screen_width,
screen_height))

#load the background image
background = pygame.image.load("background.png")

#the player
player = pygame.image.load("player_pirate.png")

#set the colour white to be transparent
player.set_colorkey((255,255,255))

#the treasure
treasure = pygame.image.load("treasure.png")

#set the colour white to be transparent
treasure.set_colorkey((255,255,255))

#used to determine if the game is running
game_is_running = True

#while the game is still running
while game_is_running:

    #for every event that happens in our game
    for event in pygame.event.get():

        #if the event is a quit event then exit
        if event.type == pygame.QUIT:
            exit()

    #draw the background at screen location 0,0
    screen.blit(background, (0,0))

    #draw the player
    screen.blit(player, (280, 210))
    screen.blit(treasure, (160, 20))

    #draw our temporary screen to the actual screen
    pygame.display.update()
```

What we have done here is tell our program that we want to create a transparent colour by using the set_colorkey function. Note that the word 'colour', in the function, 'set_color' is spelled differently and uses the American-English way of spelling the word colour. How did we arrive at the colour white? Each colour is created using a number from 0 to 255. 0 is black and the number 255 is white. Each number in the function represents a Red, Green or Blue colour. Changing these numbers allows us to mix the colours to create other colours. Remember in art class when you mixed red with some white and you created a pink colour? This same principle applies here. The image below should give you a clearer explanation.

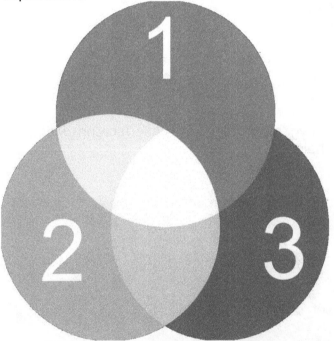

1 represents the red colour mix, 2 the green colour mix and 3 the blue colour mix. If we mix all these three colours together by increasing each of these colours to 255 (the maximum), then we create the colour white.

File name: TheTreasure.py

CHAPTER 37 - MOVING THE PLAYER

To move the player you will use the keyboard arrow keys. If you think back to chapter 8 and remember what was said about events and how they work, then you will know that we need to look for an event. That event will be a keyboard event, specifically an arrow key event. Add the following highlighted code to your program.

```
import pygame
import sys

pygame.init()

#the width and height of the screen
(screen_width, screen_height) = (400, 300)

#set up the screen size and mode and store the returned
#screen data into screen
screen = pygame.display.set_mode((screen_width,
screen_height))

#load the background image
background = pygame.image.load("background.png")

#the player
player = pygame.image.load("player_pirate.png")

#set the colour white to be transparent
player.set_colorkey((255,255,255))

#the player position
player_position_x = 280
player_position_y = 210

#the treasure
treasure = pygame.image.load("treasure.png")

#set the colour white to be transparent
```

```
treasure.set_colorkey((255,255,255))

#used to determine if the game is running
game_is_running = True

#while the game is still running
while game_is_running:

    #for every event that happens in our game
    for event in pygame.event.get():

        #if the event is a quit event then exit
        if event.type == pygame.QUIT:
            exit()


    #draw the background at screen location 0,0
    screen.blit(background, (0,0))

    #draw the player
    screen.blit(player, (player_position_x, player_position_y))
    screen.blit(treasure, (160, 20))

    #draw our temporary screen to the actual screen
    pygame.display.update()
```

Run the program and view the changes. It appears that
everything is the same. While this is correct, you have made
your program more flexible by using variables instead of static
numbers. If you want to change the position of the player,
then you can just change the variable player_position_x. This
means that if you want to move the position of the player when
a key has been pressed then you do so. Go ahead and add
the following highlighted code to your program.

```
import pygame
import sys

pygame.init()
```

```python
#the width and height of the screen
(screen_width, screen_height) = (400, 300)

#set up the screen size and mode and store the returned
#screen data into screen
screen = pygame.display.set_mode((screen_width,
screen_height))

#load the background image
background = pygame.image.load("background.png")

#the player
player = pygame.image.load("player_pirate.png")

#set the colour white to be transparent
player.set_colorkey((255,255,255))

#the player position
player_position_x = 280
player_position_y = 210

#the treasure
treasure = pygame.image.load("treasure.png")

#set the colour white to be transparent
treasure.set_colorkey((255,255,255))

#used to determine if the game is running
game_is_running = True

#while the game is still running
while game_is_running:

    #for every event that happens in our game
    for event in pygame.event.get():

        #if the event is a quit event then exit
        if event.type == pygame.QUIT:
            exit()
```

```
    if event.type == pygame.KEYDOWN:
        if event.key == pygame.K_LEFT:
            player_position_x -= 4

    #draw the background at screen location 0,0
    screen.blit(background, (0,0))

    #draw the player
    screen.blit(player, (player_position_x, player_position_y))
    screen.blit(treasure, (160, 20))

    #draw our temporary screen to the actual screen
    pygame.display.update()
```

Before I explain what these additional lines do, go ahead and run the program and press the left arrow key on your keyboard.

The highlighted code above is within the list of events that occur and this means that we can look for events that we are interested in. We want to move the player using the keyboard which means we want to look for keyboard events. If the event type is a key down event, meaning that someone has pressed a key then we want to know about it. Next, we want to check if the key that has been pressed is the left arrow key. If it is then we want to do perform some action. The pygame.K_LEFT is referring to the left arrow key and when this event happens, we are moving the player left or decreasing it's X position.

The line that makes the character move is this one.

```
    player_position_x -= 4
```

This is telling the program is to get the players X position and take away 4 from its current position. Using the image below as an example, the user has pressed the left arrow key 3 times, each time taking away the value of 4 from its current position.

The player now has the ability to move in the left direction. We will go ahead and add the additional movement. Enter the following highlight code.

```
import pygame
import sys

pygame.init()

#the width and height of the screen
(screen_width, screen_height) = (400, 300)

#set up the screen size and mode and store the returned
#screen data into screen
screen = pygame.display.set_mode((screen_width,
screen_height))

#load the background image
background = pygame.image.load("background.png")

#the player
player = pygame.image.load("player_pirate.png")
```

```python
#set the colour white to be transparent
player.set_colorkey((255,255,255))

#the player position
player_position_x = 280
player_position_y = 210

#the treasure
treasure = pygame.image.load("treasure.png")

#set the colour white to be transparent
treasure.set_colorkey((255,255,255))

#used to determine if the game is running
game_is_running = True

#while the game is still running
while game_is_running:

    #for every event that happens in our game
    for event in pygame.event.get():

        #if the event is a quit event then exit
        if event.type == pygame.QUIT:
            exit()

        if event.type == pygame.KEYDOWN:

            #if the user has pressed the left arrow key
            if event.key == pygame.K_LEFT:
                player_position_x -= 4

            #if the user has pressed the right arrow key
            elif event.key == pygame.K_RIGHT:
                player_position_x += 4

            #if the user has pressed the up arrow key
            elif event.key == pygame.K_UP:
                player_position_y -= 4
```

```
#if the user has pressed the down arrow key
elif event.key == pygame.K_DOWN:
    player_position_y += 4



#draw the background at screen location 0,0
screen.blit(background, (0,0))

#draw the player
screen.blit(player, (player_position_x, player_position_y))
screen.blit(treasure, (160, 20))

#draw our temporary screen to the actual screen
pygame.display.update()
```

Run this program and use the arrow keys to move your player around the island.

We have added the right, up and down arrow keys but instead of using the 'if' statement to determine if something has been pressed, we are using the 'elif' keyword. This is telling our program that if something didn't happen then if might be one of these. You should read the 'elif' keyword like this.
'If' the A key is pressed, else it might be the 'B' key that has been pressed.

File name: MoveThePlayer.py

CHAPTER 38 - THE TREASURE

In this chapter you will move the player until it reaches the treasure. When the player reaches the treasure the player will win and the game will be over. This addition to the game isn't reflected in our game design document, so we need to modify the document to reflect the changes. Specifically, we need to change the heading 'How to play'.

How to play

While the game is running
    If the player clicks on the red X in the window, the game will end
    If the player collides with the treasure
        exit the game
    Draw the island background
    Move the player
    Draw the player
    Draw the treasure
    If the player reaches the treasure, the player wins and the game will end
In order for the player to make contact with the treasure, add the additional highlighted lines to your program.

```
import pygame
import sys

pygame.init()

#the width and height of the screen
(screen_width, screen_height) = (400, 300)

#set up the screen size and mode and store the returned
#screen data into screen
screen = pygame.display.set_mode((screen_width,
screen_height))

#load the background image
background = pygame.image.load("background.png")
```

```python
#the player
player = pygame.image.load("player_pirate.png")

#set the colour white to be transparent
player.set_colorkey((255,255,255))

#the player position
player_position_x = 280
player_position_y = 210

#create a player bounding rectangle
player_rectangle = player.get_rect()
player_rectangle.move_ip(player_position_x,
player_position_y)

#the treasure
treasure = pygame.image.load("treasure.png")

#set the colour white to be transparent
treasure.set_colorkey((255,255,255))

#set the treasure position
treasure_position_x = 160
treasure_position_y = 20

#create a treasure bounding rectangle
treasure_rectangle = treasure.get_rect()
treasure_rectangle.move_ip(treasure_position_x,
treasure_position_y)

#used to determine if the game is running
game_is_running = True

#while the game is still running
while game_is_running:

    #for every event that happens in our game
    for event in pygame.event.get():
```

```python
    #if the event is a quit event then exit
    if event.type == pygame.QUIT:
        exit()

    if event.type == pygame.KEYDOWN:

        #if the user has pressed the left arrow key
        if event.key == pygame.K_LEFT:
            player_position_x -= 4

        #if the user has pressed the right arrow key
        elif event.key == pygame.K_RIGHT:
            player_position_x += 4

        #if the user has pressed the up arrow key
        elif event.key == pygame.K_UP:
            player_position_y -= 4

        #if the user has pressed the down arrow key
        elif event.key == pygame.K_DOWN:
            player_position_y += 4

        #set the player rectangle position
        player_rectangle.x = player_position_x
        player_rectangle.y = player_position_y

        #move the player rectangle to the same position as the
player position
        player_rectangle.move(player_position_x,
player_position_y)

        #if the player rectangle collides with the treasure rectangle
        if player_rectangle.colliderect(treasure_rectangle):

            #exit the game
            exit()

    #draw the background at screen location 0,0
    screen.blit(background, (0,0))
```

```
#draw the player
    screen.blit(player, (player_position_x, player_position_y))
    screen.blit(treasure, (treasure_position_x,
treasure_position_y))

#draw our temporary screen to the actual screen
    pygame.display.update()
```

Go ahead and run the program. Move the player up towards the treasure. As soon as the player touches the treasure, the game will exit.

In order to detect when an object has collided with another object, you will need to create rectangles that surround the objects. In our case, the objects are the player and the treasure.

File name: GetTreasure.py

The following lines are used to create a rectangle and move the rectangle into position.

```
#create a player bounding rectangle
player_rectangle = player.get_rect()
player_rectangle.move_ip(player_position_x,
player_position_y)
```

Ignoring the comment, the first actual line of code is creating a rectangle called player_rectangle and this is based on the player image dimensions. The rectangle created is the same size as the actual image. The diagram below will show the bounding rectangle.

The next line moves the rectangle into the current position where the player is positioned. In our case it will be placed at 280 in X and 210 in Y.

```
#create a treasure bounding rectangle
treasure_rectangle = treasure.get_rect()
treasure_rectangle.move_ip(treasure_position_x,
treasure_position_y)
```

The first line of code creates a bounding rectangle based on the dimensions of the treasure. Again we move the rectangle into the same location as the treasure.

```
#set the player rectangle position
player_rectangle.x = player_position_x
player_rectangle.y = player_position_y
```

Next we update the player rectangle by obtaining the players X and Y locations and assigning them to player_rectangle.x.

```
#move the player rectangle to the same position as the
player position
player_rectangle.move(player_position_x,
player_position_y)
```

We update the rectangles location after we have moved the player. We do not need to move the treasure as this is a stationary bounding rectangle.

The line below handles the collision between our player rectangle and the treasure rectangle.

```
#if the player rectangle collides with the treasure rectangle
if player_rectangle.colliderect(treasure_rectangle):

#exit the game
    exit()
```

If this bounding rectangle comes into contact with the treasures bounding box rectangle, then we can detect a collision.

The image above is demonstrating the collision between the two bounding boxes by highlighting the collision in purple. The line below returns true if a collision occurs.

```
if player_rectangle.colliderect(treasure_rectangle):
```

If the function returns true then the line below tells our program to exit.

```
    exit()
```

```
File name: TheTreasure.py
```

CHAPTER 39 - DISPLAYING THE WINNER

You have the player reaching his goal which was to find the treasure. When this happens, the game just ends. It would be nice to inform the user that they have won. We have come up with an idea which is not contained in our original game design document. We need to completely review the game design document and modify any changes that are needed.

Let's update our game design document to reflect the new ideas that we want to add.

Treasure Quest

Document version: 1.1
28/06/2012
Revision: 2
Programming: Your Name
Graphics : Your Name
Music & sound effects: None

Design History
Version 1.1. The document has been updated to reflect the new addition of a message that will be displayed when the user comes into contact with the treasure.

Overview
The game is set on a remote island in the Caribbean. The objective of this game is to control the player character and to locate the buried treasure. When the treasure is found a message will be display informing the user that he or she has won.

Gameplay
This game will be in the style of an arcade game in which the player will run around the island looking for the buried treasure. The player will control the pirate and the treasure will be a stationary image. The player will win the game as soon as the game character reaches the treasure, at which point the game will display a message. The game can be terminated if the user presses the red X on the window.

Game features
One level
One player
A map of an island
The treasure
The player character
A winning message will be displayed when the user locates
the treasure
Game characters
The player character will be a pirate.
The treasure will be a treasure check containing gold coins.
Level design
The design below uses a single screen with a single level. If
the player reaches the treasure, the player wins and a
message will be displayed. There is no way for the player to
lose.

Artwork

 The player

 The treasure

Sound and Music
None
Game controls
The game will be controlled by the user using the keyboard.
The UP, DOWN, LEFT and RIGHT arrows will be used to
move the player character around the screen.
User Interface / HUD
None. This will normally display user lives, points, score and
so on.

How to play
While the game is running
        If the player clicks on the red X in the window, the
game will end

        If the player collides with the treasure
                Display a message informing the user that he or
        she has won

        Draw the island background
        Move the player
        Draw the player
        Draw the treasure
        ~~If the player reaches the treasure, the player wins and~~
~~the game will end~~

Now that you have your game design modified, we can go
ahead and add the changes to the program.

Add the following highlighted code to your program. There is a deliberate bug in our game design document which will be reflected in the code. This has been intentionally placed in the game design document to demonstrate how important the game design process is. I want you to understand this deliberate error, as it will save you a lot of time in the future. Add the following highlighted code into your program.

```python
import pygame
import sys

pygame.init()

#the width and height of the screen
(screen_width, screen_height) = (400, 300)

#set up the screen size and mode and store the returned
#screen data into screen
screen = pygame.display.set_mode((screen_width,
screen_height))

#load the background image
background = pygame.image.load("background.png")

#the player
player = pygame.image.load("player_pirate.png")

#set the colour white to be transparent
player.set_colorkey((255,255,255))

#the player position
player_position_x = 280
player_position_y = 210

#create a player bounding rectangle
player_rectangle = player.get_rect()
player_rectangle.move_ip(player_position_x,
player_position_y)

#the treasure
```

```python
treasure = pygame.image.load("treasure.png")

#set the colour white to be transparent
treasure.set_colorkey((255,255,255))

#set the treasure position
treasure_position_x = 160
treasure_position_y = 20

#create a treasure bounding rectangle
treasure_rectangle = treasure.get_rect()
treasure_rectangle.move_ip(treasure_position_x,
treasure_position_y)

#font information
font = pygame.font.SysFont("arial", 16)
text = font.render("You win", True, (0,0,0), (255,255,255))

#used to determine if the game is running
game_is_running = True

#while the game is still running
while game_is_running:

    #for every event that happens in our game
    for event in pygame.event.get():

        #if the event is a quit event then exit
        if event.type == pygame.QUIT:
            exit()

        if event.type == pygame.KEYDOWN:

            #if the user has pressed the left arrow key
            if event.key == pygame.K_LEFT:
                player_position_x -= 4

            #if the user has pressed the right arrow key
            elif event.key == pygame.K_RIGHT:
                player_position_x += 4
```

```
        #if the user has pressed the up arrow key
        elif event.key == pygame.K_UP:
            player_position_y -= 4

        #if the user has pressed the down arrow key
        elif event.key == pygame.K_DOWN:
            player_position_y += 4

        #set the player rectangle position
        player_rectangle.x = player_position_x
        player_rectangle.y = player_position_y

        #move the player rectangle to the same position as the
player position
        player_rectangle.move(player_position_x,
player_position_y)

    #if the player rectangle collides with the treasure rectangle
    if player_rectangle.colliderect(treasure_rectangle):
        #display the text
        screen.blit(text, (0,0))

    #draw the background at screen location 0,0
    screen.blit(background, (0,0))
    #draw the player
    screen.blit(player, (player_position_x, player_position_y))
    screen.blit(treasure, (treasure_position_x,
treasure_position_y))

    #draw our temporary screen to the actual screen
    pygame.display.update()
```

Before I show you where the bug will appear, let's first go over
the new additional lines.

```
#font information
font = pygame.font.SysFont("arial", 16)
text = font.render("You win", True, (0,0,0), (255,255,255))
```

We want to display a message on the screen informing the user that they have won. In order to do this, we need to create a font object as we will be displaying text. We create the Arial style font which is 16 pixels. We then create a variable called, '*text*'. Normally this would be more informative such as '*winning_text*' or '*you_win_text*', but as this is the only text we want to display, we will just call it text.

The font.render function will accept a string, which will be the message we want to be displayed. In this case, the message is "You win". Next we pass in a '*true*' value, which tells the function to create a smooth looking message. This is called anti-aliasing. You can turn this off by passing in the value of 'false'. The next two sets of values passed in are the fore colour and the background colour. You should remember that from our discussion on colours that (0,0,0) is black and (255,255,255) is white. We are instructing our program to display black text on a white background.

Finally we want to replace the following lines when the bounding rectangles collide.

```
#if the player rectangle collides with the treasure rectangle
if player_rectangle.colliderect(treasure_rectangle):
    #display the text
    screen.blit(text, (0,0))
```

Here we are displaying or blitting the text image to the screen at location 0,0. This will appear in the top left location of our game window.

Now run the program and move the game character towards the treasure. When the player is touching the treasure, a message should be displayed. It appears that our message isn't being displayed. The message is being displayed but we can't see it. Why is this? This has to do with the way the images are being drawn or to be exact, the order in which they are drawn.

Examine the following code.

```
if player_rectangle.colliderect(treasure_rectangle):
    #display the text
    screen.blit(text, (0,0))

    #draw the background at screen location 0,0
    screen.blit(background, (0,0))
    #draw the player
    screen.blit(player, (player_position_x, player_position_y))
    screen.blit(treasure, (treasure_position_x,
treasure_position_y))
```

The order in which the game is being drawn is like this,
assuming that the rectangles are not colliding.

- Draw the background
- Draw the player
- Draw the treasure

This is fine as we want all our images to be drawn on top of
the background. The problem arises when we have a
collision. The orders in which the images are drawn have
changed.

The sequence now looks like this.
- Draw the text
- Draw the background
- Draw the player
- Draw the treasure

We are drawing the 'You win' message first and then we are
drawing the background over the top followed by the rest of
the game objects. We need to change this order so that the
text appears on top of all the game objects.

Again we need to modify our game design document. At this point you should realise why it is sometimes called a living document due to the constant updates. I have left out the revision changes and I am just concentrating on the How to play section, but you should update the revision history every time the document has been modified.

How to play
While the game is running
　　　If the player clicks on the red X in the window, the game will end
　　　Draw the island background
　　　Move the player
　　　Draw the player
　　　Draw the treasure

If the player collides with the treasure
　　　Display a message informing the user that he or she has won

Change the program so that it looks like the following.

```
import pygame
import sys

pygame.init()

#the width and height of the screen
(screen_width, screen_height) = (400, 300)

#set up the screen size and mode and store the returned
#screen data into screen
screen = pygame.display.set_mode((screen_width,
screen_height))

#load the background image
background = pygame.image.load("background.png")

#the player
player = pygame.image.load("player_pirate.png")
```

```python
#set the colour white to be transparent
player.set_colorkey((255,255,255))

#the player position
player_position_x = 280
player_position_y = 210

#create a player bounding rectangle
player_rectangle = player.get_rect()
player_rectangle.move_ip(player_position_x,
player_position_y)

#the treasure
treasure = pygame.image.load("treasure.png")

#set the colour white to be transparent
treasure.set_colorkey((255,255,255))

#set the treasure position
treasure_position_x = 160
treasure_position_y = 20

#create a treasure bounding rectangle
treasure_rectangle = treasure.get_rect()
treasure_rectangle.move_ip(treasure_position_x,
treasure_position_y)

#font information
font = pygame.font.SysFont("arial", 16)
text = font.render("You win", True, (0,0,0), (255,255,255))

#used to determine if the game is running
game_is_running = True

#while the game is still running
while game_is_running:

    #for every event that happens in our game
    for event in pygame.event.get():
```

```python
    #if the event is a quit event then exit
    if event.type == pygame.QUIT:
        exit()

    if event.type == pygame.KEYDOWN:

        #if the user has pressed the left arrow key
        if event.key == pygame.K_LEFT:
            player_position_x -= 4

        #if the user has pressed the right arrow key
        elif event.key == pygame.K_RIGHT:
            player_position_x += 4

        #if the user has pressed the up arrow key
        elif event.key == pygame.K_UP:
            player_position_y -= 4

        #if the user has pressed the down arrow key
        elif event.key == pygame.K_DOWN:
            player_position_y += 4

        #set the player rectangle position
        player_rectangle.x = player_position_x
        player_rectangle.y = player_position_y

        #move the player rectangle to the same position as the
player position
        player_rectangle.move(player_position_x,
player_position_y)

    #draw the background at screen location 0,0
    screen.blit(background, (0,0))

    #draw the player
    screen.blit(player, (player_position_x, player_position_y))
    screen.blit(treasure, (treasure_position_x,
treasure_position_y))
```

```
#if the player rectangle collides with the treasure
rectangle
  if player_rectangle.colliderect(treasure_rectangle):
    #display the text
    screen.blit(text, (0,0))

    #draw our temporary screen to the actual screen
  pygame.display.update()
```

We have now moved the 'you win' text below the other images
that have been drawn. This places our message on top of all
the images.

Run the program and view the result.

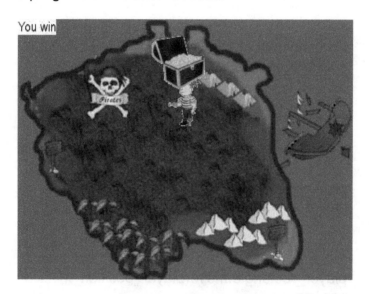

CHAPTER 40 - THE MESSAGE

The message is now being displayed in the top left corner of the game screen. Although this is working, it's not great. We need to modify the program so that the message displayed is displayed larger and in the centre of the screen. Go ahead and modify the program so that it looks like the following program below.

```
import pygame
import sys

pygame.init()

#the width and height of the screen
(screen_width, screen_height) = (400, 300)

#set up the screen size and mode and store the returned
#screen data into screen
screen = pygame.display.set_mode((screen_width,
screen_height))

#load the background image
background = pygame.image.load("background.png")

#the player
player = pygame.image.load("player_pirate.png")

#set the colour white to be transparent
player.set_colorkey((255,255,255))

#the player position
player_position_x = 280
player_position_y = 210

#create a player bounding rectangle
player_rectangle = player.get_rect()
player_rectangle.move_ip(player_position_x,
player_position_y)
```

```python
#the treasure
treasure = pygame.image.load("treasure.png")

#set the colour white to be transparent
treasure.set_colorkey((255,255,255))

#set the treasure position
treasure_position_x = 160
treasure_position_y = 20

#create a treasure bounding rectangle
treasure_rectangle = treasure.get_rect()
treasure_rectangle.move_ip(treasure_position_x,
treasure_position_y)

#font information
font = pygame.font.SysFont("arial", 28)
text = font.render("You win", True, (0,0,0), (255,255,255))

#used to determine if the game is running
game_is_running = True

#while the game is still running
while game_is_running:

    #for every event that happens in our game
    for event in pygame.event.get():

        #if the event is a quit event then exit
        if event.type == pygame.QUIT:
            exit()

        if event.type == pygame.KEYDOWN:

            #if the user has pressed the left arrow key
            if event.key == pygame.K_LEFT:
                player_position_x -= 4

            #if the user has pressed the right arrow key
```

```python
        elif event.key == pygame.K_RIGHT:
            player_position_x += 4

        #if the user has pressed the up arrow key
        elif event.key == pygame.K_UP:
            player_position_y -= 4

        #if the user has pressed the down arrow key
        elif event.key == pygame.K_DOWN:
            player_position_y += 4

        #set the player rectangle position
        player_rectangle.x = player_position_x
        player_rectangle.y = player_position_y

        #move the player rectangle to the same position as the
player position
        player_rectangle.move(player_position_x,
player_position_y)

        #draw the background at screen location 0,0
        screen.blit(background, (0,0))

        #draw the player
        screen.blit(player, (player_position_x, player_position_y))
        screen.blit(treasure, (treasure_position_x,
treasure_position_y))

        #if the player rectangle collides with the treasure
rectangle
        if player_rectangle.colliderect(treasure_rectangle):
            #display the text
            screen.blit(text, (screen_width / 2, screen_height / 2))

        #draw our temporary screen to the actual screen
        pygame.display.update()
```

The font size has now been change to 28 pixels and we used
some maths calculations to position the, 'You win' message.

We take the value of the screen_width, which is 400 and we divide this by 2. This gives us the value of 200. This positions the start of the message at 200 pixels from the left of the screen. We do the same with the height of the screen by also dividing this by 2. The screen_height is 300 which when divided by 2, gives us the result of 150 pixels. This places the start of the text 150 pixels from the top of the screen.
Run the program and observe the result.

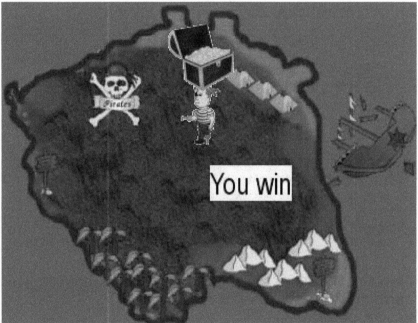

The result should look like the image above. The only problem is that the message starts in the centre which makes the, 'You win' message look as though it is off centre. We need to adjust the start position in X. We can do this by allowing Pygame to do some more calculations for us. Modify the line in which we are adding the 'You win' message.

```
#if the player rectangle collides with the treasure
rectangle
   if player_rectangle.colliderect(treasure_rectangle):
       #display the text
       screen.blit(text, (screen_width / 2 - 50, screen_height /
2))
```

This line is now displaying our text followed by a calculation to position the start of the text. We first take the screen_width value, divide it by 2 and take away 50. This calculation, when broken down will look like this.

```
400 / 2 = 200
200 – 50 = 150
```

The message looks far better than it did previously.

File name: GetTreasureDisplayMessage.py

CHAPTER 41 - SMOOTHER MOVEMENT

A movement problem with the character still exists. Every time the key is pressed, it only moves the character 4 pixels and stops. What we really want to do is to constantly move the character while the key is being held down. Our game design document does not need any modification because our document specified that we only want to move the character using the keyboard. We didn't' mention anything about how smooth it should move. Modify the following highlighted line in the program.

```
import pygame
import sys

pygame.init()

#the width and height of the screen
(screen_width, screen_height) = (400, 300)

#set up the screen size and mode and store the returned
#screen data into screen
screen = pygame.display.set_mode((screen_width,
screen_height))

#load the background image
background = pygame.image.load("background.png")

#the player
player = pygame.image.load("player_pirate.png")

#set the colour white to be transparent
player.set_colorkey((255,255,255))

#the player position
player_position_x = 280
player_position_y = 210

#create a player bounding rectangle
```

```python
player_rectangle = player.get_rect()
player_rectangle.move_ip(player_position_x,
player_position_y)

#the treasure
treasure = pygame.image.load("treasure.png")

#set the colour white to be transparent
treasure.set_colorkey((255,255,255))

#set the treasure position
treasure_position_x = 160
treasure_position_y = 20

#create a treasure bounding rectangle
treasure_rectangle = treasure.get_rect()
treasure_rectangle.move_ip(treasure_position_x,
treasure_position_y)

#font information
font = pygame.font.SysFont("arial", 28)
text = font.render("You win", True, (0,0,0), (255,255,255))

#used to determine if the game is running
game_is_running = True

pygame.key.set_repeat(50, 50)

#while the game is still running
while game_is_running:

    #for every event that happens in our game
    for event in pygame.event.get():

        #if the event is a quit event then exit
        if event.type == pygame.QUIT:
            exit()

        if event.type == pygame.KEYDOWN:
```

```python
        #if the user has pressed the left arrow key
        if event.key == pygame.K_LEFT:
            player_position_x -= 4

        #if the user has pressed the right arrow key
        elif event.key == pygame.K_RIGHT:
            player_position_x += 4

        #if the user has pressed the up arrow key
        elif event.key == pygame.K_UP:
            player_position_y -= 4

        #if the user has pressed the down arrow key
        elif event.key == pygame.K_DOWN:
            player_position_y += 4

        #set the player rectangle position
        player_rectangle.x = player_position_x
        player_rectangle.y = player_position_y

        #move the player rectangle to the same position as the
player position
        player_rectangle.move(player_position_x,
player_position_y)

    #draw the background at screen location 0,0
    screen.blit(background, (0,0))

    #draw the player
    screen.blit(player, (player_position_x, player_position_y))
    screen.blit(treasure, (treasure_position_x,
treasure_position_y))

        #if the player rectangle collides with the treasure
rectangle
    if player_rectangle.colliderect(treasure_rectangle):
        #display the text
        screen.blit(text, (screen_width / 2 - 50, screen_height /
2))
```

```
#draw our temporary screen to the actual screen
pygame.display.update()
```

Run the program and hold an arrow key down. You will notice that the pirate continuously moves around the screen. What we have told our program that we want keys to be repeated. The first value in the pygame.key.set_repeat function informs set_repeat to delay 50 milliseconds before it checks which key has been pressed again. The next value is how often the KEYDOWN event will be sent in milliseconds. To get an idea of how this works, go ahead and change the line that reads

```
pygame.key.set_repeat(50, 50)
```

to

```
pygame.key.set_repeat(950, 50)
```

Run the program and hold down an arrow key. You should notice a slight delay before the pirate character starts to move. Now modify the line that reads

```
pygame.key.set_repeat(950, 50)
```

to
```
pygame.key.set_repeat(50, 950)
```

Run the program and hold down the arrow key. You will notice that the pirate character moves very slowly. This is because we have increased the second value to 950 milliseconds. This value is how often Pygame will check to see if a user has pressed a key.

Go ahead and change the line that reads

```
pygame.key.set_repeat(50, 950)
```

back to its original values.

```
pygame.key.set_repeat(50, 50)
```

File name: SmoothMovement.py

CHAPTER 42 - MUSIC AND SOUND FX

The final touch to this small game is to add some music which will play in the background and then add some sound effects. Before we can start programming, we need to go back to our game design document and add the additional game information.

Treasure Quest

Document version: 1.2
28/06/2012
Revision: 3
Programming: Your Name
Graphics : Your Name
Music & sound effects: None

Design History
Version 1.1. The document has been updated to reflect the new addition of a message that will be displayed when the user comes into contact with the treasure.

Version 1.2. The document has been updated to reflect the new addition of music and sound effects.
Overview
The game is set on a remote island in the Caribbean. The objective of this game is to control the player character and to locate the buried treasure. When the treasure is found a message will be display informing the user that he or she has won. Music will play in the background and the game will contain sound effects.
Gameplay
This game will be in the style of an arcade game in which the player will run around the island looking for the buried treasure. The player will control the pirate and the treasure will be a stationary image. The player will win the game as soon as the game character reaches the treasure, at which point the game will display a message. The game can be terminated if the user presses the red X on the window.

Game features
One level
One player
A map of an island
The treasure
The player character
Background music
Sound Effects for the player when moving
Game characters
The player character will be a pirate.
The treasure will be a treasure check containing gold coins.
Level design
The design below uses a single screen with a single level. If the player reaches the treasure, the player wins and a message will be displayed. There is no way for the player to lose.

Artwork

 The player

 The treasure

Sound Effects and Music
Music will play at the start of the game and will continue while the player does not exit the game
A step sound will be played every time the player moves the character. This will simulate the player walking on the island.
Game controls
The game will be controlled by the user using the keyboard. The UP, DOWN, LEFT and RIGHT arrows will be used to move the player character around the screen.
User Interface / HUD
None. This will normally display user lives, points, score and so on.

How to play
Play background music
While the game is running
        If the player clicks on the red X in the window, the game will end
        Draw the island background
        Move the player position
        Draw the player
        Play step sound

        Draw the treasure

If the player collides with the treasure
        Display a message informing the user that he or she has won
                Play winning sound

Now the game design document has been modified, we can move on to our program changes. We will start by adding the sound effects when the pirate character walks. Make the following changes to your program.

```
import pygame
import sys


pygame.init()

#initialise the mixer
pygame.mixer.init()

#the width and height of the screen
(screen_width, screen_height) = (400, 300)

#set up the screen size and mode and store the returned
#screen data into screen
screen = pygame.display.set_mode((screen_width,
screen_height))

#load the background image
background = pygame.image.load("background.png")

#the player
player = pygame.image.load("player_pirate.png")

#set the colour white to be transparent
player.set_colorkey((255,255,255))

#the player position
player_position_x = 280
player_position_y = 210

#create a player bounding rectangle
player_rectangle = player.get_rect()
player_rectangle.move_ip(player_position_x,
player_position_y)

#load the player steps
```

```python
steps= pygame.mixer.Sound("steps.ogg")

#the treasure
treasure = pygame.image.load("treasure.png")

#set the colour white to be transparent
treasure.set_colorkey((255,255,255))

#set the treasure position
treasure_position_x = 160
treasure_position_y = 20

#create a treasure bounding rectangle
treasure_rectangle = treasure.get_rect()
treasure_rectangle.move_ip(treasure_position_x,
treasure_position_y)

#font information
font = pygame.font.SysFont("arial", 28)
text = font.render("You win", True, (0,0,0), (255,255,255))

#used to determine if the game is running
game_is_running = True

#set the keyboard repeats
pygame.key.set_repeat(50, 50)

#while the game is still running
while game_is_running:

    #for every event that happens in our game
    for event in pygame.event.get():

        #if the event is a quit event then exit
        if event.type == pygame.QUIT:
            exit()

        if event.type == pygame.KEYDOWN:

            #if the user has pressed the left arrow key
```

```python
            if event.key == pygame.K_LEFT:
                player_position_x -= 4
                steps.play()

            #if the user has pressed the right arrow key
            if event.key == pygame.K_RIGHT:
                player_position_x += 4
                steps.play()


            #if the user has pressed the up arrow key
            if event.key == pygame.K_UP:
                player_position_y -= 4
                steps.play()


            #if the user has pressed the down arrow key
            if event.key == pygame.K_DOWN:
                player_position_y += 4
                steps.play()

            #set the player rectangle position
            player_rectangle.x = player_position_x
            player_rectangle.y = player_position_y

            #move the player rectangle to the same position as the
player position
            player_rectangle.move(player_position_x,
player_position_y)

        #draw the background at screen location 0,0
        screen.blit(background, (0,0))

        #draw the player
        screen.blit(player, (player_position_x, player_position_y))
        screen.blit(treasure, (treasure_position_x,
treasure_position_y))

            #if the player rectangle collides with the treasure
rectangle
        if player_rectangle.colliderect(treasure_rectangle):
```

```
#display the text
    screen.blit(text, (screen_width / 2 - 50, screen_height /
2))

#draw our temporary screen to the actual screen
pygame.display.update()
```

Run the program and move your pirate character around the screen using the arrow keys. As your pirate character moves, you will hear the sounds of footsteps rustling in the leaves. First we have to tell our program that we want to use music and sound effects. In order to do this, we use the following line to initialise Pygame to use sound.

```
#initialise the mixer
pygame.mixer.init()
```

So now that we have everything set up to start loading our sound effects let's start to load our foot step sound from an audio file. The file we are using is called 'steps.ogg'. Ogg is an audio file format that we will be using and is much like an mp3 file format. The following line of code loads this file using the, 'Pygame.mixer.Sound' function. You pass to this function the name of the file you want to use, in our case 'steps.ogg'.

```
#load the player steps
steps= pygame.mixer.Sound("steps.ogg")
```

When the file is loaded into memory, it is stored in the 'steps' variable which we will use later.

```
    if event.key == pygame.K_LEFT:
        player_position_x -= 4
        steps.play()

    #if the user has pressed the right arrow key
    if event.key == pygame.K_RIGHT:
        player_position_x += 4
        steps.play()
```

```
#if the user has pressed the up arrow key
if event.key == pygame.K_UP:
    player_position_y -= 4
    steps.play()

#if the user has pressed the down arrow key
if event.key == pygame.K_DOWN:
    player_position_y += 4
    steps.play()
```

When the user presses any of the arrow keys then we want to create the effect of the pirate walking in the undergrowth. When the user does press an arrow key, we use the steps.play() function to play the sound.

The next thing we need to add is the background music. There is a difference with the background music in that we want the music to play for long as the game is running. Add the following highlighted lines of code.

```
import pygame
import sys


pygame.init()

#initialise the mixer
pygame.mixer.init()

#the width and height of the screen
(screen_width, screen_height) = (400, 300)

#set up the screen size and mode and store the returned
#screen data into screen
screen = pygame.display.set_mode((screen_width,
screen_height))
```

```python
#load the background image
background = pygame.image.load("background.png")

#the player
player = pygame.image.load("player_pirate.png")

#set the colour white to be transparent
player.set_colorkey((255,255,255))

#the player position
player_position_x = 280
player_position_y = 210

#create a player bounding rectangle
player_rectangle = player.get_rect()
player_rectangle.move_ip(player_position_x,
player_position_y)

#load the player steps
steps= pygame.mixer.Sound("steps.ogg")

##load the music
music = pygame.mixer.Sound("music.ogg")

#the treasure
treasure = pygame.image.load("treasure.png")

#set the colour white to be transparent
treasure.set_colorkey((255,255,255))

#set the treasure position
treasure_position_x = 160
treasure_position_y = 20

#create a treasure bounding rectangle
treasure_rectangle = treasure.get_rect()
treasure_rectangle.move_ip(treasure_position_x,
treasure_position_y)

#font information
```

```python
font = pygame.font.SysFont("arial", 28)
text = font.render("You win", True, (0,0,0), (255,255,255))

#used to determine if the game is running
game_is_running = True

#set the keyboard repeats
pygame.key.set_repeat(50, 50)

#play the music forever
music.play(-1)

#while the game is still running
while game_is_running:

    #for every event that happens in our game
    for event in pygame.event.get():

        #if the event is a quit event then exit
        if event.type == pygame.QUIT:
            exit()

        if event.type == pygame.KEYDOWN:

            #if the user has pressed the left arrow key
            if event.key == pygame.K_LEFT:
                player_position_x -= 4
                steps.play()

            #if the user has pressed the right arrow key
            if event.key == pygame.K_RIGHT:
                player_position_x += 4
                steps.play()


            #if the user has pressed the up arrow key
            if event.key == pygame.K_UP:
                player_position_y -= 4
                steps.play()
```

```
        #if the user has pressed the down arrow key
        if event.key == pygame.K_DOWN:
            player_position_y += 4
            steps.play()

        #set the player rectangle position
        player_rectangle.x = player_position_x
        player_rectangle.y = player_position_y

        #move the player rectangle to the same position as the
player position
            player_rectangle.move(player_position_x,
player_position_y)

        #draw the background at screen location 0,0
        screen.blit(background, (0,0))

        #draw the player
        screen.blit(player, (player_position_x, player_position_y))
        screen.blit(treasure, (treasure_position_x,
treasure_position_y))

        #if the player rectangle collides with the treasure
rectangle
        if player_rectangle.colliderect(treasure_rectangle):
            #display the text
            screen.blit(text, (screen_width / 2 - 50, screen_height /
2))

        #draw our temporary screen to the actual screen
        pygame.display.update()
```

Run the program and you should hear the background music being played. When you move the pirate around the island, you will also hear the footsteps.

```
##load the music
music = pygame.mixer.Sound("music.ogg")
```

We are loading the 'music.ogg' and storing this sound in our 'music' variable. Next, we want to play this music before the game starts but after the game has been setup and initialised.

```
#play the music forever
music.play(-1)
```

The line of code above will appear just above the game loop. The -1 value which is passed into the play function will cause the music to play in a continuous loop.

```
File name: SoundsEffects.py
```

CHAPTER 43 - THE GAME LOOP EXPLAINED

We have been using a game loop but as yet I haven't really explained in detail why we need it. You can think of a game loop as something that will keep repeating until the player wins, loses or exits the game. Game loops are at the heart of almost all games because without one the game would either only be played once and end or the game program would become very large.

The diagram below gives you a brief idea of how a game loop is used. You should already have a basic understanding as you have been using them since Chapter 8. Specifically we have been using it when we have the following line.

```
#used to determine if the game is running
While game_is_running:
```

The game loop can contain lots of actions and calculations, for example, the image below shows some simple actions that might take place.

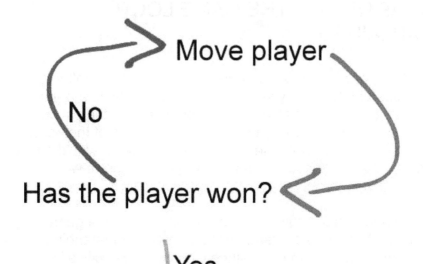

In the example above, we are moving a player and then we are checking if the player has won. If the answer is no, then we follow the blue arrow and repeat. This is the game loop. Inside a game loop a lot of other actions can take place. If it is a football game, it might check to see if the player has scored a goal or if the time is up. In the example above, if the player has won then the game has ended.

Remember: Game loops are used in all games even in games like Fifa 12, Call of Duty and Mario Kart.

Now that you understand how game loops work, we will go through a step by step guide. No programming is required in this chapter as this is only used to reinforce your understanding of a game loop.
game_playing = True

We have created a game_playing variable and we have assigned the word True to it.

Remember: A variable is something that you name that can store numbers, letters, words or even pirates in. You can think of it as a box that we can put things in such as homework, football shoes or skipping ropes.

game_playing = True

A variable called
game_playing

The game_playing variable is storing the value of True. This means that while we are playing the game, this will always contain the value True. If we stop playing the game, then game_playing will be set to False. game_playing = False. In the image below, the game_playing variable now stores the value of False.

game_playing = False

A variable called
game_playing

Now that the game_playing variable contains the value of 'False', the game loop will stop and the game will break out of the loop. So far, we haven't discussed what happens when the player exits the game by pressing X on the window.

The image below has set the game_playing to 'True', which creates our game loop. Anything that appears indented where the red arrow appears will be repeated in the game loop.

```
1    import pygame
2
3    pygame.init()
4    window = pygame.display.set_mode((500, 500))
5    pygame.display.set_caption("Treasure Quest by Scott Wren")
6
7    game_playing = True
8
9
10   while game_playing :
11
12
13          ---->
```

The image below demonstrates in plain English how the game loop will work. It starts at the top of the while loop and while this is true, the indented words will be executed. The player is moved, the dog is moved and the cat is moved. The next line performs an 'if' statement check. If the player has pressed the space bar, then 'the game is playing' is set to 'False'. The loop will evaluate the loop.

This will cause the loop to exit because when the while statement is tested, the 'game playing' is now false. The while loop will not run and the program skips this entire loop and moves down to the line that reads, 'Display the game has finished'.

while the game is playing:
    Move player
    Move dog
    Move cat

    If the player has pressed space bar then
        set while game is playing to 'False'

Display the game has finished

CHAPTER 44 - THE SCREEN BOUNDARY

The final touch to this simple game is to stop the pirate player from moving out of the playing area. This can be done by checking to see if the player has moved out of the game area in the game loop. If the player is out of the area, then we can stop the playing from moving any further.
We will need to update our game design document again to reflect these changes. The document should look like this.

Treasure Quest

Document version: 1.3
28/06/2012
Revision: 4
Programming: Your Name
Graphics : Your Name
Music & sound effects: None

Design History
Version 1.1. The document has been updated to reflect the new addition of a message that will be displayed when the user comes into contact with the treasure.

Version 1.2. The document has been updated to reflect the new addition of music and sound effects.
Version 1.3. The document has been updated so that the player can no longer move off the playing area.
Overview
The game is set on a remote island in the Caribbean. The objective of this game is to control the player character and to locate the buried treasure. When the treasure is found a message will be display informing the user that he or she has won. Music will play in the background and the game will contain sound effects.

Gameplay

This game will be in the style of an arcade game in which the player will run around the island looking for the buried treasure. The player will control the pirate and the treasure will be a stationary image. The player will win the game as soon as the game character reaches the treasure, at which point the game will display a message. The game can be terminated if the user presses the red X on the window.

Game features

One level

One player

A map of an island

The treasure

The player character

Background music

Sound Effects for the player when moving

Game characters

The player character will be a pirate.

The treasure will be a treasure check containing gold coins.

Level design
The design below uses a single screen with a single level. If the player reaches the treasure, the player wins and a message will be displayed. There is no way for the player to lose. The player is not allowed to move out of the screen.

Artwork

  The player

  The treasure

Sound Effects and Music
Music will play at the start of the game and will continue while the player does not exit the game
A step sound will be played every time the player moves the character. This will simulate the player walking on the island.
Game controls
The game will be controlled by the user using the keyboard. The UP, DOWN, LEFT and RIGHT arrows will be used to move the player character around the screen.

User Interface / HUD
None. This will normally display user lives, points, score and so on.

How to play
Play background music
While the game is running
If the player clicks on the red X in the window, the game will end
If the player moves out of the playing area, then stop the player from moving off the screen
Draw the island background
Move the player position
Draw the player
Play step sound
Draw the treasure

If the player collides with the treasure
Display a message informing the user that he or she has won
Play winning sound

Now that the game design document has been updated, we can go ahead and modify the code. Add the following highlighted code.

```python
import pygame
import sys


pygame.init()

#initialise the mixer
pygame.mixer.init()

#the width and height of the screen
(screen_width, screen_height) = (400, 300)

#set up the screen size and mode and store the returned
```

```python
#screen data into screen
screen = pygame.display.set_mode((screen_width,
screen_height))

#load the background image
background = pygame.image.load("background.png")

#the player
player = pygame.image.load("player_pirate.png")

#set the colour white to be transparent
player.set_colorkey((255,255,255))

#the player position
player_position_x = 280
player_position_y = 210

#create a player bounding rectangle
player_rectangle = player.get_rect()
player_rectangle.move_ip(player_position_x,
player_position_y)

#load the player steps
steps= pygame.mixer.Sound("steps.ogg")

##load the music
music = pygame.mixer.Sound("music.ogg")

#the treasure
treasure = pygame.image.load("treasure.png")

#set the colour white to be transparent
treasure.set_colorkey((255,255,255))

#set the treasure position
treasure_position_x = 160
treasure_position_y = 20

#create a treasure bounding rectangle
treasure_rectangle = treasure.get_rect()
```

```python
treasure_rectangle.move_ip(treasure_position_x,
treasure_position_y)

#font information
font = pygame.font.SysFont("arial", 28)
text = font.render("You win", True, (0,0,0), (255,255,255))

#used to determine if the game is running
game_is_running = True

#set the keyboard repeats
pygame.key.set_repeat(50, 50)

#play the music forever
music.play(-1)

#while the game is still running
while game_is_running:

    #for every event that happens in our game
    for event in pygame.event.get():

        #if the event is a quit event then exit
        if event.type == pygame.QUIT:
            exit()

        #if the player hits the left side of the screen
        if player_position_x < 0:
            player_position_x = 0

        #if the player hits the right side of the screen
        if player_position_x > screen_width -
player_rectangle.width:
            player_position_x = screen_width -
player_rectangle.width

        #if the player hits the top of the screen
        if player_position_y < 0:
            player_position_y = 0
```

```python
#if the player hits the bottom of the screen
    if player_position_y > screen_height -
player_rectangle.height:
        player_position_y = screen_height -
player_rectangle.height


    if event.type == pygame.KEYDOWN:

        #if the user has pressed the left arrow key
        if event.key == pygame.K_LEFT:
            player_position_x -= 4
            steps.play()

        #if the user has pressed the right arrow key
        if event.key == pygame.K_RIGHT:
            player_position_x += 4
            steps.play()


        #if the user has pressed the up arrow key
        if event.key == pygame.K_UP:
            player_position_y -= 4
            steps.play()

        #if the user has pressed the down arrow key
        if event.key == pygame.K_DOWN:
            player_position_y += 4
            steps.play()

        #set the player rectangle position
        player_rectangle.x = player_position_x
        player_rectangle.y = player_position_y

        #move the player rectangle to the same position as the
player position
        player_rectangle.move(player_position_x,
player_position_y)

    #draw the background at screen location 0,0
```

```
        screen.blit(background, (0,0))

        #draw the player
        screen.blit(player, (player_position_x, player_position_y))
        screen.blit(treasure, (treasure_position_x,
treasure_position_y))

        #if the player rectangle collides with the treasure
rectangle
        if player_rectangle.colliderect(treasure_rectangle):
            #display the text
            screen.blit(text, (screen_width / 2 - 50, screen_height /
2))

        #draw our temporary screen to the actual screen
        pygame.display.update()
```

Examine the code below.

```
        #if the player hits the left side of the screen
        if player_position_x < 0:
            player_position_x = 0
```

This line of code will check to see if the player_position_x, is
less than 0. If it is then it means that the pirate is about to go
out of our playing area. This line only checks the left boarder
of our playing area. We will have to check each side of game
area. Checking the right side of the game area is a little
trickier.

```
        #if the player hits the right side of the screen
        if player_position_x > screen_width -
player_rectangle.width:
            player_position_x = screen_width -
player_rectangle.width
```

The above code reads like this. If the current position of the player in the X coordinate is greater than the screen width, minus the width of the player rectangle then set the player position to the screen width minus the width of the player rectangle.

Take a look at the maths behind the idea and then take a look at the diagram which will make it clearer.
Screen Width – Width of the player rectangle
   400   - 30   = 370

This means that our pirate character will stop at position 370 in the X position. This is exactly what we need. We want it to appear as though the right side of the character is bumping into the edge of the screen.

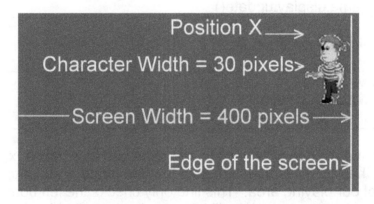

If we didn't calculate the width of the pirate character, then the character would actually move off the screen and then the character would stop moving.

Remember that the X position of the pirate character is calculated from the left hand side of the game character. The image below is showing what would happen if we didn't calculate the width of the character.

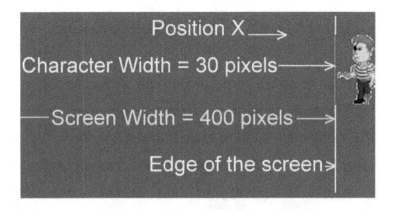

The Y positions of the pirate character use the same principle.

```
#if the player hits the top of the screen
if player_position_y < 0:
    player_position_y = 0
```

If the Y position of the game character has reached the top of the screen, then set the player position to 0. Again we are using the players Y position to see if the pirate has reached the bottom of the screen. Remember that we have to calculate the character height.

```
#if the player hits the bottom of the screen
        if player_position_y > screen_height -
player_rectangle.height:
            player_position_y = screen_height -
player_rectangle.height
```

CHAPTER 45 - THE ECLIPSE IDE

The use of an IDE program can be far easier than working with nano or some other generic text editor. An IDE contains a suite of tools that will help the programmer recognise typos, make suggestions and aid in visually debugging your code. Eclipse is one of the best editors available because it can be used on multiple platforms and can integrate multiple languages and compilers from Python, C++ to java and can even be used when developing android applications and games.

To install eclipse enter the following commands and make sure that you are a root user

```
# yum install eclipse
```

When eclipse has installed you can start it by going to 'Applications→Development→Eclipse'.

Eclipse will display a splash screen while it is loading and you will be presented with a window containing the location of your workspace. The workspace location will be where your source code will be stored. Source code is the term given to code that you will write.

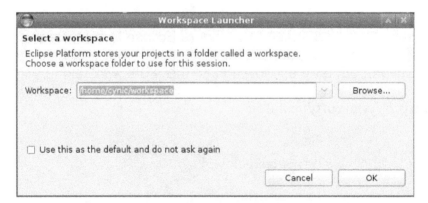

Click OK to accept the default location. Eclipse will then display a welcome screen with some options. It is recommended that you go through the tutorials after you have read this so that you are familiar with Eclipse and its options.

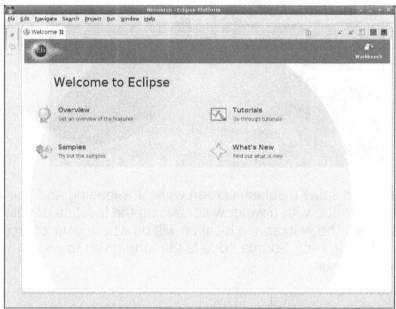

The first thing you need to configure Eclipse is to locate the PyDev plugin. Go to the Help menu and select 'Install New Software'. Enter the following into the 'work with' textbox.

http://pydev.org/updates

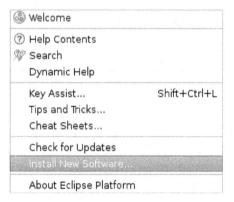

Click on the *Add* button and another window will appear asking you to enter a name. Enter *PyDev* and in the location field enter

http://pydev.org/updates

Eclipse will search the PyDev web site for available plugins. After a few minutes you should be presented with the following screenshot.

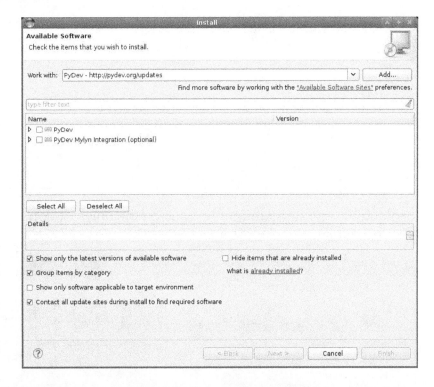

Select the arrow next to PyDev and check the box labelled *PyDev for Eclipse* and clicked on the next button.

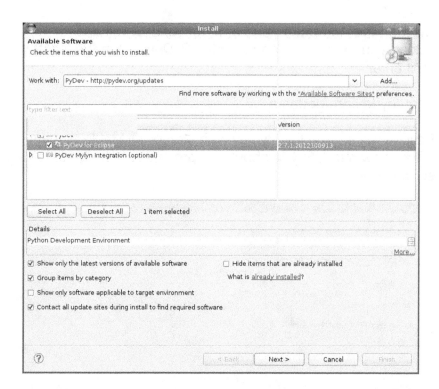

Accept the license agreement and click on the finish button.
PyDev will continue to download and install.

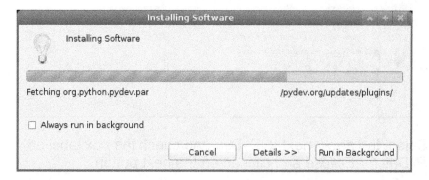

A warning window will pop up informing you that you are
installing software that contains unsigned content. Click OK to
accept this. Select the checkbox that says Aptana PyDev and
click OK.

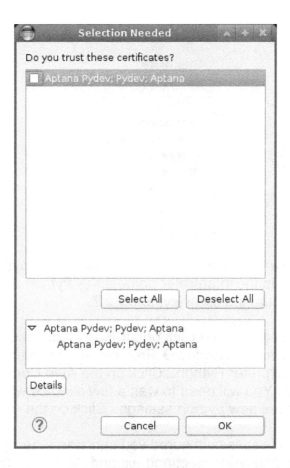

You will need to restart eclipse for the changes to take effect.

Next you will need to configure eclipse so that it can locate the python interpreter. Go to Window→Preferences and select PyDev→Interpreter - Python.

Select the *New* button and enter the path to the python interpreter. In the interpreter name enter *Python 2.7*, assuming your version of Python is 2.7.

Go to File→New→ and click on the Project menu item. Open in the menu Window→ Preference and select Pydev→Interpreter Python. Click on the *Auto Config* button, click *Apply.* You will need to wait a few minutes while eclipse configures the new python settings. Click on the *OK* button.

Now that Eclipse is configured you can start a new project. Select File→New→Project and expand the PyDev folder and click on PyDev Project. You will also notice a number of other project types that can be created here including the *PyDev Google App Engine Project* and the PyDev Django Project. PyDev Project is the only one we are concerned with here.

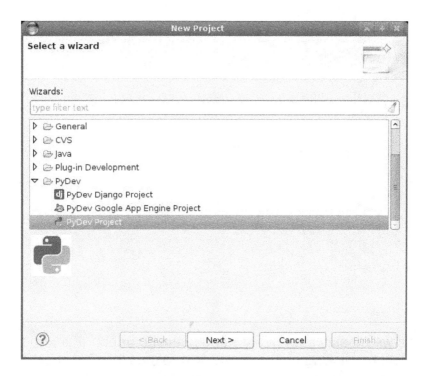

Enter a new project name called HelloRaspberryPi. Make sure Python is selected as the project type and select the grammar type of 2.6 or later. Select *Python* for the interpreter type. Leave the other settings as they are and click on the *finish* button. Another window will be displayed asking you if you want a PyDev perspective click on the *Yes* button.

Click on the *Workbench* icon located on the right hand side.

This will display the PyDev working environment. Expand the project by clicking on the arrow next to the HelloRaspberryPi folder.

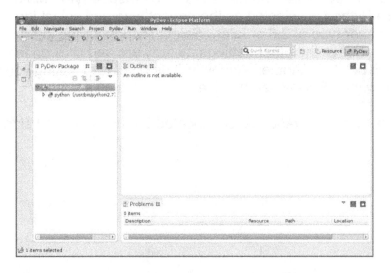

Right click on the HelloRaspberryPi folder and select *New→File.*

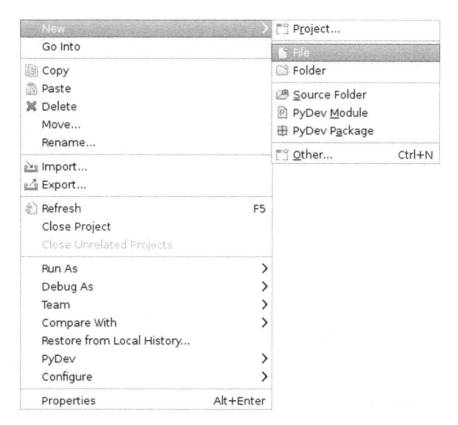

Enter the name of the file as *hello.py* and click on the *Finish* button. If the new window is obscuring the window behind it, click on the *restore* button to lock the window in place.

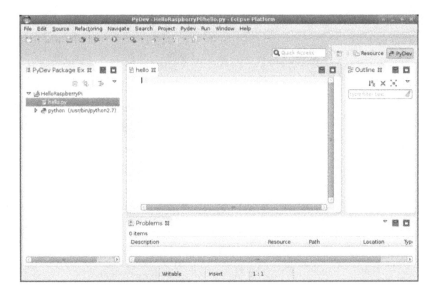

You should now have a blank file displayed. Copy the contents below into this file.

```
greetings = "Hello Raspberry Pi"
print(greetings)
```

To run this program you will need to click on the green icon shown below.

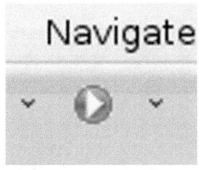

This will produce a window with a title of *Run As. Python Run* should already be highlighted so click on the *OK* button.

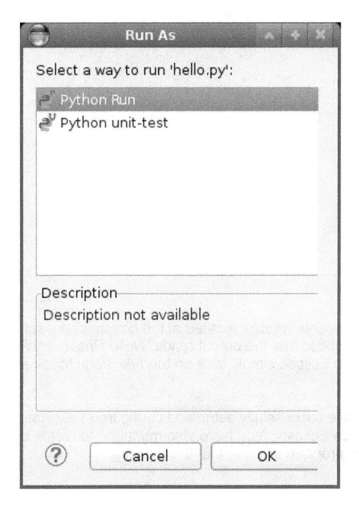

The next window should already have the *hello.py* file selected. Click on the *OK* button.

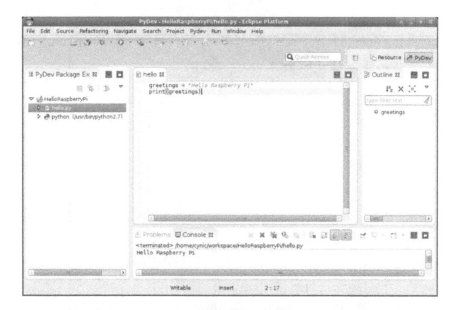

In the console window located at the bottom of the screen you should notice that the output reads "*Hello Raspberry Pi*". To exit from Eclipse simply click on the *File* menu followed by the exit item.

You have successfully setup and configured your Raspberry Pi to use Eclipse. You have also managed to create a very simple program to verify that it is working.

PART 4
THE EXTRA BITS

CHAPTER 46 - RASPBERRY PI REVISION 2

Revision 2 of the Raspberry Pi was created to address some minor issues that have been known to cause problems. Most of these issues wouldn't have been noticed because they are non-critical issues. Some of the changes are at a technical level and will not affect your daily use. Other changes include modifications to the General Purpose Input Output (GPIO). These pins are used so that you can use your Raspberry Pi with external devices such as LEDs, motors and various input devices.

Other changes include fixes that caused problems for some users when using the HDMI output. A +5V0 leak over the HDMI connection was reported when the Raspberry Pi was plugged into some TV's. Revision 2 also has mounting holes to keep it stable when fitting it into a case. It is important to note that these changes are minor and do not contain anything like a new processor or additional memory. To determine if you have a revision 2 board enter the following

$ cat /proc/cpuinfo

The information returned will be similar to this.

Processor : ARMv6-compatible processor rev 7 (v6l)
BogoMIPS : 697.95
Features : swp half thumb fastmult vfp edsp java tls
CPU implementer : 0x41
CPU architecture: 7
CPU variant : 0x0
CPU part : 0xb76
CPU revision : 7

Hardware : BCM2708
Revision : 0004
Serial : 000000009a5d9c2f

The important line in the above output is the line that reads:
Revision : 0004

If your revision number is 0004 or greater then you have a model B revision 2.0 Raspberry Pi. Any number less than this will be a model B revision 1.0.

The Raspberry Pi is able to you communicate with the outside world by using the General Purpose Input Output or GPIO for short. The GPIO is a set of pins on the Raspberry Pi which allow you to send and receive signals. They are called general purpose because there is no specific function for these pins. These 26 pins are circled in red below.

17 of these pins can be used for input and output. Before you can start using the GPIO port you will need additional components which can consists of breadboards for connecting circuits, wires, LEDs, resistors and other electronic components. If using electronic components are not your cup of tea you can always look at other devices designed specifically for interfacing with the outside world. One such device is called Pi-Face which we will use for a simple project later in this chapter.

You can damage your Raspberry Pi if you are unsure of what you are doing. It is recommended that you use an expansion board such as Pi-Face or the Gertboard as this will add the protection that is needed when using GPIO otherwise you could damage your Raspberry Pi.

The following steps are not an in depth discussion on electronics or the components but rather a general overview of the steps required in order to get started with GPIO. For more information on how to get started with electronics for the Raspberry Pi I suggest that you browse the internet for various projects aimed at using electronics. When you have a completed circuit you will generally follow the steps below. Before embarking on your journey of electronics you will need to identify which revision of the Raspberry Pi you have. At the time of writing this book there are 2 revisions of the Raspberry Pi available. Each revision has a slightly different pin layout which can lead to some confusion.

The diagrams below highlight the changes between the two revisions.

Revision 1

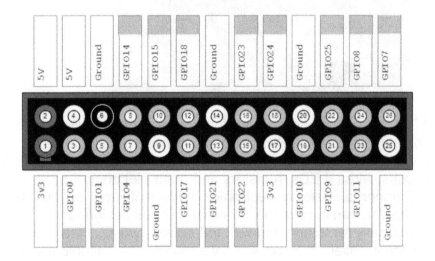

Revision 2

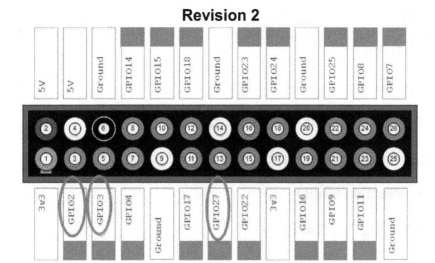

Revision 2 changes are highlighted in red.

Your next step will be to use a programming language or Scratch to interface with the GPIO pins. If you plan on programming and using the GPIO port then you have a number of libraries at your disposal. Probably the most common library is the raspberry-gpio-python library. You must have python installed to use the raspberry-gpio-python library. If you do not have python installed see "Python Programming" in the previous chapter.

Open a terminal window and enter the following.

$ sudo mkdir gpio

Followed by

$ cd gpio

Next we need to download the RPi.GPIO library. The current version available when writing this book is version 0.4.1a. Enter the following command all on one line.

$ wget
http://pypi.python.org/packages/source/R/RPi.GPIO/RPi.GPIO
-0.4.1a.tar.gz

Enter

$ tar xzvf RPi.GPIO-0.4.1a.tar.gz

This will extract the contents to a new library.

Go ahead and enter

$ cd RPi.GPIO-0.4.1a

Next we need to install the library into python. Enter the following

$ sudo python setup.py install

Now that the library has been installed you can start using it but first you will have to write a program to see any results.

Enter the following

$ nano piflash.py

The following program will make use of the GPIO pins by flashing an LED. In order for you to see the result of this program you will need to have LEDs wired up to the appropriate pins.

Remember that this is only a guide to the steps involved.

The code below will send an output signal to pins 15 and 16.

The first step is to import the RPi library into your program. The Raspberry Pi needs to know if you are setting a pin to be used as an input or an output. In the program below we are using GPIO.setup(15, GPIO.OUT) to setup pin 15 to be used as an output pin. The rest of the program uses GPIO.output to turn the LEDs on and off.

```
from time import sleep
import RPi.GPIO as GPIO

GPIO.setup(15, GPIO.OUT)
GPIO.setup(16, GPIO.OUT)

while 1:
        GPIO.output(15, False)
        sleep(2)

        GPIO.output(15, True)
        sleep(2)

        GPIO.output(16, False)
        sleep(2)

        GPIO.output(16, True)
        sleep(2)
```

Save the file and at the terminal enter

```
$ sudo python piflash.py
```

CHAPTER 47 - PIFACE

Pi-Face is an interface device that plugs directly into the GPIO pins and allows you to use the Raspberry Pi to send and receive signals. You can use the Raspberry Pi to signal the Pi-Face device to power motors, controls lights, sensors etc. This resolves the problem of wiring components such as LEDs, switches etc and will allow you to start testing code right away. This option is still available if required.

Pi-Face Digital Interface

LEDs
The Pi-Face device has a total of 4 onboard red LEDs that are connected to pins 1-4 on the Pi-Face device.

Buttons
Pi-Face has a total of 8 pins for input and 8 pins for output. You will find 4 buttons that are connected to the input pins 1 to 4. These buttons are complete the circuit when the button is pushed down.

Relays

The Pi-Face is equipped with 2 relays that are connected to the output pins 1 and 2. This is useful for controlling different voltage items.

This image shows the Pi-Face Digital Device connected to the Raspberry Pi.

Connect your Pi-Face board to the Raspberry Pi as per the instructions supplied by the University of Manchester and download the following Raspberry Pi image which has everything you need to get started with Pi-Face. The following image can be downloaded from Manchester University using the following url.

http://pi.cs.man.ac.uk/download/

Burn the image to an SD card and boot up your Raspberry Pi. Use the following details to login.

'pi' for the login name.
'raspberry' for the password.

Enter

$ python

To test Pi-Face we will import the Pi-Face library. Enter the following.

```
>>> import piface.pfio as pfio
```

Next we need to initialize PiFace.

```
>>> pfio.init()
```

You may hear a click which indicates that your program has initialized Pi-Face. To actually see some type of result enter the following to turn on the red LED.

```
>>> pfio.LED(1).turn_on()
>>> pfio.LED(2).turn_on()
```

If you take a look at your Pi-Face device you will notice that 2 red LEDs are lit up. To turn the LEDs off enter

```
>>> pfio.LED(1).turn_off()
>>> pfio.LED(2).turn_off()
```

Hold down the control key and press D to exit. Now that the Pi-Face device is working we can now go ahead and write a short program using Python. Enter the following to create a file using the nano editor.

```
$ nano buttontest.py
```

```
import piface.pfio as pfio

#initialize piface
pfio.init()
```

```
#create a loop that will go on forever
while True:

        #read the input from each button
        button1 = pfio.digital_read(1)
        button2 = pfio.digital_read(2)
        button3 = pfio.digital_read(3)
        button4 = pfio.digital_read(4)

        #if button1 has been pressed then turn on LED1
        if button1 == True:
                pfio.digital_write(1, 1)

        #if button2 has been pressed then turn on LED2
        if button2 == True:
                pfio.digital_write(2, 1)
        #if button3 has been pressed then turn off LED1
        if button3 == True:
                pfio.digital_write(1, 0)

        #if button4 has been pressed then turn off LED2
        if button4 == True:
                pfdio.digital_write(2, 0)
        sleep(.25)
```

The code above first imports the Pi-Face library which gives
you the ability to use Pi-Face. The line that reads 'as pfio' is
used because it allows us to reference Pi-Face using just 'pfio'
instead of typing 'piface.pfio' each time. Pi-Face is initialized
using the 'pfio.init()' method. A while loop is created that will
never end and inside this loop we are checking to see if any of
the 4 buttons on the Pi-Face device are pressed. This is
checked by using the '*pfio.digital_read(1)*' for button 1. If any
of the buttons have been pressed then a button variable is set
to true. Next we determine which button has been set to true
by using an 'if' statement. If this comparison is found to be
true then we turn the LED on or off depending on which button
was pressed.

The line that reads pfdio.digital_write(1, 1) will turn the first red LED on. Here we are using the digital_write method which accepts two parameters. The first parameter is used to indicate which LED to write to and the second parameter is used to turn the LED on or off, 1 being on and 0 being off.

CHAPTER 48 - BERRYBOOT

Berryboot will allow you to install multiple operating systems on the same SD card or a hard drive. This is great for testing applications across multiple platforms and allows you to simply boot from one operating system to the next.

To install Berryboot download the latest zip file from the source forge from the following location.

http://sourceforge.net/projects/berryboot/files/

The current version available when writing this is berryboot-20130213.zip.

Insert a FAT32 formatted SD card into your computer. I am using Windows 7 in the example below but the process is similar depending no matter which operating system you are using. Extract the contents to a folder and drag all the files to the SD card.

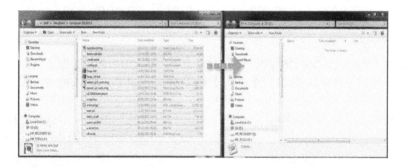

When the files have copied across to the SD card, remove the card from your computer and insert it into your Raspberry Pi. Plug in an Ethernet cable into your Raspberry Pi and make sure it is connected to the internet. The reason for this is that Berryboot will allow you to download operating systems from the Internet.

Plug in the power adapter to your Raspberry Pi.

The first screen that appears will allow you to adjust some installation settings. One of the options available is to disable overscan if you see any green borders.

Select if you are using a wired connection or a Wi-Fi connection. Select your time zone and keyboard layout. Next select the destination drive or SD card. If you have a large enough SD card you should select mmcblk0: SD0xyz. Note that the xyz will be the size of your card in gigabytes. You also have some extended features below that allow you to change the file system type and to encrypt the contents on the SD card or hard drive. For now leave the settings set to *ext4 (no trim/discard)* and make sure that *Encrypt disk* is unchecked. Click on the *Format* button.

After a few seconds you will see a list of operating systems available for your Raspberry Pi. Select an operating system and click on *download*. When the operating system has completed you should click on the exit menu item. This will exit Berryboot and allow the selected the operating system to boot.

If you need to add another operating systems reboot the Raspberry Pi and select *Edit* from the Berryboot screen. Click on the *Add OS* icon at the top of the window. This will display the available operating systems menu. Follow the same procedure to install additional operating systems. If you want an operating system to boot by default then all you need to do is select the operating system from the list and select the star icon.

What next?

There are a number of things that you can do with your Raspberry Pi including electronics, home automation, creating games and more. You have at your disposal an amazing piece of hardware which will allow you to understand the Linux operating system, use applications and create web sites. This is just a short list of possibilities. Your next step really depends on your interests. If you are looking to become a web designer or web programmer then you should look at Wordpress and PHP as a starting point. If you are trying to get into programming then you should start with Python. If games are your thing then take a look at Pygame. If music and audio is your thing then try one of the music trackers available. For graphics you should take a look at GIMP. If you just want a cheap general day to day production computer then try Libre office.

The possibilities are limited by your knowledge. Enjoy the journey.

Acknowledgements

I would like to acknowledge George Williams, The Debian Project, The Free Software Foundation, The Open Clip Art Library, Linus Torvalds, and Jeff Minter at Llamasoft and everyone that has made the Raspberry Pi such an inspiration.